Hebrew Academy of West Queens

To give every Jewish  *n,*
no matter wha
and make them and the שומרי תו...

A lofty goal, no doubt, yet critical to the survival of the Jewish nation in these turbulent and rapidly changing times.

Since opening its doors in 1965, the Hebrew Academy of West Queens has provided thousands of children with a Torah-true education.

In addition to a full Yeshiva curriculum featuring superior Jewish and secular studies divisions, the Hebrew Academy operates a specialized and highly successful outreach program. Remedial classes, private tutoring and social services are offered to former public school students, as well as to Soviet, Iranian and Israeli emigres.

Unique in its approach, the program blends the new with the old, the recently arrived with the veteran yeshiva student, to facilitate a quick and effective transition into the school's mainstream classes.

Each year, hundreds of foreign children find new life within the Yeshiva's caring environment. Its dedicated staff members have inspired many to embrace our beautiful heritage and become outstanding members of the American Jewish community.

88-01 102nd Street / Richmond Hill N.Y. 11418 / (718) 847-1462

לזכר נשמת

ר׳ דוד בן חיים הלל קסטרוויצקי זצ״ל

In loving memory of Peshy's father,
Reb Dovid Kastrovitzky

and

לזכר נשמת

ר׳ אברהם אלטר בן טוביה קורץ ע״ה

In loving memory of Shloimie's father,
Reb Alter Kurz

יודע ד׳ ימי תמימים ונחלתם לעולם תהי׳
תהלים יז:יח
"Hashem knows the days of
those who are wholehearted
and their inheritance shall be forever."

May our children be imbued with the love of learning
which their grandfathers זצ״ל so faithfully embraced.

Peshy and Shloimie Katz

In Honor of

Brenda Gubin

Sidney and Sally Gubin

Sam and Eleanor Gubin

Joseph and Ethel Bender

Ben and Anna Beitch

Herbert and Florence Stein

Morris and Tillie Feinhause

In their זכות we should

see the return of all כלל ישראל

to תורה ומצות

Joel and Arleen Gubin

Bayla Burke

לזכר נשמת

ר׳ יצחק מרדכי בן ר׳ יוסף חיים הכהן

In Loving Memory

of

Isi Adest

The Adest Family

לזכר נשמת

In memory of
our beloved and esteemed
friend and colleague

Paul Mittel

ר׳ יששכר ב״ר דניאל הלוי

שנלב״ע בערב שבת נחמו נחמו עמי
ט״ו באב תשנ״ב

Who served as Vice President
of our Yeshiva for many years
with dedication, total commitment,
personal involvement and sacrifice.

Hebrew Academy of West Queens

Mr. Bernard Zyniewski, President

Mr. Ludwig Katz, Vice President

Mr. Jerry Ornstein, Treasurer

Mrs. Iris Fein, Secretary

Rabbi Moshe Stahler, Dean

Rabbi Aaron Scholar, Administrator

In Memory of

Morris and Anna Hulkower

Louis and Rose Zyniewski

Lee Zyniewski

Libby Alperowitz

Helen Goodman

Sarah Schurman

Dedicated in Cherished Memory of our

Dear Son and Brother

Michael Ross Feurman

A loving heart and Ben Torah

and a complete joy

to all who were privileged to know him.

During his brief lifetime he brought us

only nachas and happiness.

The Feurman Family

כי אם בתורת ה׳ חפצו ובתורתו יהגה יומם ולילה

His desire is in the Torah of Hashem
and in his Torah he meditates day and night.

לזכר נשמות

ר' יוסף בן ר' יעקב ע"ה

מרת פייגא בת ר' יעקב ע"ה

ר' חיים יהושע בן ר' דוד ע"ה

מרת חנה בת ר' משה הכהן

מרת שרה פייגא בת ר' חיים יהושע ע"ה

ר' משה אהרן בן ר' דוד הלוי ע"ה

In Loving Memory of

Joseph and Fanny Leitner

Hyman and Anna Stahler

Sandra Fay Stahler

Morris Zharnest

Their lifelong dedication to Torah education
continues to be an inspiration to us
their children and grandchildren

Rabbi and Mrs. Moshe Stahler
and Yosefa
Rabbi and Mrs. David Zharnest
Shira Chaya, Aharon Yehoshua
Yitzchok Yosef and Chana Fayge
Mr. and Mrs. Yaakov Stahler

לזכר נשמות

חיה בת ר׳ אליעזר הלוי סראלאוויטש

ר׳ נפתלי בן ר׳ רפאל פרוידינבערגער

אסתר בת ר׳ יחיאל מיכל ווינקלער

May their exemplary lives of devotion to Torah

and chesed be an inspiration to their children,

grandchildren and great grandchildren

Mr. and Mrs. Allen Szrolovits

and Family

In Memory of
our beloved parents

Mr. Joseph Leitner ע״ה

Mrs. Fanny Leitner ע״ה

Mrs. Edith Prager ע״ה

Who taught us, guided us,
and inspired us בדרך התורה
so that we could do the same
for our children.

Shmuel and Yocheved Prager

לזכר נשמות

אבא מורי

אברהם אבא בן אהרן אליעזר
סקאלער ע״ה

אמא מורתי

האשה חיה בת דוד הכהן
סקאלער ע״ה

In Memory of

Max Hecht
מרדכי בן ר׳ שמואל העכט ע״ה

ArtScroll Series®

Rabbi Nosson Scherman / Rabbi Meir Zlotowitz

General Editors

Published by

Mesorah Publications, ltd

RABBI YISROEL MILLER

*Provocative and penetrating
insights on the Festivals,
Purim and Chanukah*

FIRST EDITION
First Impression . . . March 1998

Published and Distributed by
MESORAH PUBLICATIONS, Ltd.
4401 Second Avenue
Brooklyn, New York 11232

Distributed in Europe by
J. LEHMANN HEBREW BOOKSELLERS
20 Cambridge Terrace
Gateshead, Tyne and Wear
England NE8 1RP

Distributed in Israel by
SIFRIATI / A. GITLER — BOOKS
10 Hashomer Street
Bnei Brak 51361

Distributed in Australia & New Zealand by
GOLDS BOOK & GIFT CO.
36 William Street
Balaclava 3183, Vic., Australia

Distributed in South Africa by
KOLLEL BOOKSHOP
Shop 8A Norwood Hypermarket
Norwood 2196, Johannesburg, South Africa

ISBN
1-57819-183-1 (hard cover)
1-57819-184-X (paperback)

Typography by Compuscribe at ArtScroll Studios, Ltd.

Printed in the United States of America by Noble Book Press
Bound by Sefercraft, Quality Bookbinders, Ltd. Brooklyn, N.Y.

TABLE OF CONTENTS

INTRODUCTION:

I Promised Rav Shneur zt"l

t was the winter *zman* (term) of 5738, January 1978. After seven and a half years of learning in Beth Medrash Govoha of Lakewood, New Jersey, I was leaving with a group of friends to help found a *kollel* in Pittsburgh, Pennsylvania. The yeshivah made a *seudas preidah* for us, a farewell party in the dining hall replete with cake and speeches, and I was called upon to say a few words.

After expressing my feelings as to what the years in the yeshivah had meant to me — feelings that grow only stronger with the passage of decades — I shared several thoughts that for some time had been weighing on my mind. In those days I was rash and stupid (since then, I have succeeded in becoming cautious and stupid), and with bull-in-a-china-shop delicacy I began talking about a somewhat sensitive subject. I don't have a transcript, but the talk went something like this:

"There is a problem in the yeshivah that some *talmidim* (students) have, in that some of the *talmidim* do not appreciate the *shmuessin* (talks) of the *Rosh Yeshivah, shlita*. They think that the *shmuess* tends to ramble on; they don't see a clear structure with a formal beginning, middle and end; and if they want insights in *Tanach* or *Midrashim*, they feel they can get the information from *sefarim* (books) without coming to a *shmuess* lasting half an hour or longer.

"I would suggest that the real problem is that some of the *talmidim* do not really understand the nature of what a *shmuess* is. To offer a *mashal*, an analogy, the composer Beethoven wrote a piece of music depicting a specific battle that had taken place between the armies of England and France.

"If you listen to that piece of music, expecting to learn all about the battle, hard facts, you will be greatly disappointed. From the music you would not learn when or where the battle was fought. You would discover neither the names of the commanders, nor how many soldiers fought under their command, nor how many died. For almost anything you would want to know about the battle, you would get much more from reading a history book.

"But if what you want is to learn what battle *is*; if you want to discover what war is, what struggle is, what it means to fight and give all you have for loyalty, as part of a group banded together to do the same, *that* kind of knowledge does not come from books, and it cannot be conveyed in orderly rows of nouns and adjectives. That kind of knowledge comes only when it touches your heart, and it communicates itself in forms such as Beethoven's music. You can find facts in a library; but for the essence, the subtle core of feelings, books must give way to music, which alone can do the job.

"And the *nimshal* (lesson) is: With a *sefer* and a good *chavrusa* (study partner), you can learn Torah anywhere. But as the *Rosh Yeshivah shlita* has taught us, a yeshivah is much more than a collection of *sefarim* and *chavrusos*. As the *Rosh Yeshivah* has said so many times, to learn in the yeshivah is to be 'besoch he'anan' (inside the clouds, referring to the Clouds of Divine Glory which protected Israel in the Wilderness and elevated them to a unique spiritual status, one of the *Rosh Yeshivah*'s favorite metaphors for the atmosphere of an authentic yeshivah).

"How does one become a full part of the yeshivah, to enter the world of being *besoch he'anan*? What are the thoughts, what are the feelings, how do we learn to breathe an atmosphere that is not like anything else in this world, because it is not really *of* this world?

"Those are questions every yeshivah man must ask. But the answers are not found in *sefarim*. They are *Torah sheb'al peh* and *Toras halev*, Oral Torah and Torah of the heart. To communicate them, the *rebbi* must use not a lecture and not a *shiur*, but verbal music, and expressions of verbal color that paint a picture in words. The words must come from the *lev* and from the *neshamah*, heart and soul, and instead of a formal talk the *rebbi* speaks almost as if he were just thinking out loud; or, what we call, a *shmuess*.

"This is what the *Rosh Yeshivah shlita* does for us in his *shmuessin*, and it is one of the many things we will miss when we leave."

A day or two later, the *Rosh Yeshivah*, Rav Shneur Kotler *zt"l*, called me in. I had visions of being thrown out of the yeshivah for impertinence, even though I was already leaving. Aside from the delicate nature of the content of my talk, there was also the matter of language — I had been the first *talmid* in living memory to speak publicly in English rather than Yiddish. But instead, the *Rosh Yeshivah* thanked me for my talk, and asked if I would write it out in the form of an essay, for publication. I stammered my agreement and my thanks, received his blessing, and I and my family went off to Pittsburgh.

It was a busy year. Settling into a new community, a new *kollel*, then a new baby, with one thing after another I never did get around to writing the essay I had promised Rav Shneur. Until now.

The essays in this volume are not *shmuessin*. Each chapter has (or is at least supposed to have) a beginning, middle and end, and any perceived rambling is not for spiritual reasons. But in its own small way, each chapter is an attempt to help the reader develop feelings for things which are not easily expressed in words, though they are things which touch our hearts, and which endure.

The essays are not for the purpose of providing a "*gut vort,* good word," (*bon mot*) to "say over" at the Yom Tov table. Instead, each chapter explores some point which connects us with the central message of the Yom Tov. The reader will discover some new ideas, and — even better — some new insights into old ideas, which with Hashem's help will bring us to a deeper understanding of Yom Tov, and a deeper understanding of ourselves.

Rav Nosson Tzvi Finkel of Slabodka *zt"l* once asked Rav Yisroel Salanter *zt"l* what should the goal of today's yeshivos be (another version is that he asked what should the focus of a *mashgiach,* the yeshivah's dean of students and spiritual supervisor, be). Rav Yisroel replied with the words of the prophet, "*lehachayos lev nidkaim, lehachayos ruach shefalim,* to give life to those whose hearts are crushed, to give life to those whose spirits are low" (*Isaiah* 57:15). In seeking the message of Yom Tov, this volume also focuses on finding the message of *chizuk,* encouragement and optimism. Yom Tov is a time to rejoice, and it is hoped that readers will find thoughts of *simchah* in these pages, to give strength to themselves and to share with family and friends.

My heartfelt thanks to Miss Rosella (Rivka) Freedman of Pittsburgh, who has sponsored this volume in memory of her parents; to my nephew Rabbi Yehuda Leib Klein and his wife Esther, who for two summers gave me their home in Lakewood, New Jersey, in which to complete the manuscript; to Mrs. Peggy Safren of Lakewood, for her devoted work as unpaid research assistant; to Mrs. Judi Dick whose sensitive and professional editing enhanced this work tremendously; to my wife Debbie, without whom nothing good in my life would ever get done at all; and a special acknowledgment of my daughters Brocha and Elisheva, without whom this book might have been completed in half the time.

Y.M.
Tu B'Shvat 5758

SHALOSH REGALIM — THE THREE FESTIVALS

DONKEY LESSONS

Some people are too smart for their own good. Take Bilam, for instance. A contemporary of Moshe Rabbeinu, respected by the pagans as a prophet and sorceror, Bilam was hired by King Balak of Moab to put a curse on Israel. He knew he could not succeed without Hashem's acquiescence, and Hashem had made it clear that cursing Israel was not on the agenda; but Bilam thought he was clever enough to fool Hashem (Rashi to Numbers 22:9), so he made the attempt.

Bilam set off on his donkey to meet King Balak, and Hashem sent an angel with a sword to stand in his path. Bilam did not sense the presence of the angel, but the donkey did, and the donkey was terrified (as to what the donkey actually "saw," look at the commentary of *Ramban*). The donkey ran off the road, and Bilam began beating it. Forced into a narrow passageway, the donkey pushed Bilam's leg against a wall, and Bilam struck it again. Finally, the donkey lay down in its place, and the enraged Bilam struck it a third time.

Then: "And Hashem opened the mouth of the donkey, and it said to Bilam, 'What have I done to you, that you struck me these three times?'" (*Numbers* 22:28). That is a reasonable question for a victimized donkey; but *Midrash Tanchuma*, cited by *Rashi*, explains that the donkey meant something more. The words "three times" in Hebrew are "*shalosh regalim,*" and *Rashi* writes that, "It hinted to him: You are seeking to uproot a nation that celebrates three pilgrimage festivals (*shalosh regalim*) each year."

Imagine you were a donkey (if you prefer, you could imagine you were an angel putting words in the mouth of the donkey, but I want to make it easier for you). Is this the message you would have chosen, that Bilam seeks to uproot a nation that celebrates *shalosh regalim*, Pesach, Shavuos and Succos? What does it mean?

The simple explanation is that the donkey was trying to impress upon Bilam the enormity of his crime, that he had chosen as his target the people who serve Hashem. But if that is the meaning, why use the example of *shalosh regalim* rather than Shabbos or *tzedakah* or any other mitzvah? (To suggest that it was constrained by the need to select a mitzvah that would fit into its double entendre is a lack of understanding of the ways of the Torah and of *Chazal*, our Sages.)

And if there is indeed some reason why Yom Tov is superior to all other mitzvos, isn't it odd to focus on the aspect of Yom Tov of *shalosh regalim*, three *pilgrimage* festivals? At this time the Jewish people were still encamped together in the Wilderness, and the act of *pilgrimage*, to travel to the Sanctuary three times a year for Yom Tov, was hardly the major mitzvah event it became when our ancestors were subsequently settled and scattered on their lands in *Eretz Yisrael.* Of all the Yom Tov mitzvos, why stress *regalim*?

One of the great lessons we learn from *Chumash* is the amazing ability of human beings to be awed and elevated by a holy encounter, and then, when the encounter ends, to walk away from it as if nothing had happened. Israel witnessed the miracles of Ten Plagues and the Exodus, and just days later they said at the Red Sea, "better to have stayed in Egypt." They committed themselves to "all that Hashem has spoken we will do and we will hear," and they then heard Hashem's voice speaking to them directly, but 40 days later they danced around a golden calf.

There are many more examples, and the problem is still with us today. There are non-Orthodox Jewish organizations who run summer camps filled with "*ruach*," lots of Jewish enthusiasm, and the kids love it; and then they return to the suburbs unchanged, looking forward to being Jewish again, next summer. Even among Torah people: A young man went to hear a fiery *mussar*-talk given by a prominent Torah teacher, and afterwards he shared his enthusiasm for the teacher's no-holds-barred approach with me: "He really gave it to them," the young man said. "Them."

As a result of this problem, a hallmark of our Torah teachers has always been their insistence on learning from an experience, and taking something of it with them when they leave — "learning for the sake of doing" (*Avos* 6:6). "It is clear from the words of our Sages that if someone learned *Chumash*, for example, and did not take from it some lesson in *yiras shamayim* (fear of Heaven) or good conduct, it is not called learning at all" (*Michtav MeEliyahu*, vol. IV p.58). And the watchword of Torah-talks in the great yeshivos at the close of Yom Tov has always been, "*Vos bleibt?*" What remains with us as Yom Tov ebbs away?

Moshe Rabbeinu lived his life this way, and when he came upon the burning bush, he said: "I will turn to *see* ... why will the bush not be consumed?" (*Exodus* 3:3). Self-absorbed Bilam, on the other hand, not only did not stop to wonder about his loyal donkey's bizarre behavior, but when the donkey *spoke* to him, Bilam responded without missing a beat! This is the meaning of Bilam's later confession to the angel, "I sinned, for I did not know you stood before me" (*Numbers* 22:34), the sin of not looking for the meaning of what was happening to him (*Rav Avigdor Miller*).

Because it is so vital for us to "get the point" of what we experience, and to take it with us afterwards, the Torah gave us the mitzvah of *shalosh regalim*, to visit the *Beis Hamikdash* (Holy Temple) three times a year. "Three times during the year shall all your menfolk appear before the face of the Master, Hashem" (*Exodus* 23:17); the Torah is making clear what we are to gain from the experience, i.e., that we are servants of the Master.

As to what we took with us afterwards: One of the tithes taken from the produce in *Eretz Yisrael* was *maaser sheni* (second tithe). The farmer and his family could eat the tithed produce themselves, but it had to be eaten in the place of the Sanctuary. When the farmer came to Jerusalem on the three *regalim* to pay his respects to the Master, he brought with him his *maaser sheni* to consume during his stay, and he absorbed the unique atmosphere of the Holy City. The effect was: "that you will learn to fear Hashem your G-d all the days" (*Deuteronomy* 14:23); *all* the days, even after you leave.

So the donkey told Bilam: "Three times I have led you on a merry chase, and three times your only reaction has been to strike out blindly at me. You have learned nothing, and have not even stopped to ask what might be happening to you. And yet you hope to destroy a people who have a complete spiritual program of *shalosh regalim*, three times a year of national inspiration reminding them that they stand before the Master, and taking that awareness with them when they leave? Bilam, whatever spiritual talent you may possess, you are so completely lacking in the strength that *Klal Yisrael* has, that your quest to destroy them will never succeed."

We no longer have the blessing of *shalosh regalim*. But even today, as we enter the Sanctuary in Time that is Yom Tov to meet the Master (*moed* means a time of meeting, like the word *vaad*, a council), we can pause to remind ourselves why we have come. And even today, before we take leave of Yom Tov we can also ask, *Vos bleibt?* What will remain? What one lesson (if not more than one) can we take with us, so that donkeys will not put us to shame; so that we can assert that we are still the people who celebrate *shalosh regalim*, the special times whose effects stay with us *kal hayamim*, all the days, all our lives?

SOME THOUGHTS FOR HALLEL

The Hebrew language has many synonyms for the English word "praise," each one with its own shade of meaning. Rav Avigdor Miller points out that the word Hallel is related to mehollal, "wildness" ("lischok amarti mehollal, I said of laughter, 'It is mere wildness,'" Ecclesiastes 2:2), and "Hallel" means "praising with wild abandon," unrestrained enthusiasm. "Ish lephi mehalla-lo, a man according to his praise," (Proverbs 27:21) means that we know who a man is, not by hearing what he pays lip service to, but by seeing which things he speaks of with wild enthusiasm (automobiles and football, or mitzvos and Torah study, etc.); and Klal Yisrael reserves its Hallel for Hashem.

"*Halleluyah! Hallelu avdei Hashem*, Halleluyah! Give unrestrained praise, you servants of Hashem" (*Psalms* 113:1). To be called a servant of Hashem is a rare honor indeed, a title given in the Torah to Moshe Rabbeinu and to very few others. But when we come together on Yom Tov or Rosh Chodesh to say Hallel — and even one Jew alone is saying his or her Hallel together with other Jews around the world — each of us becomes part of something much bigger and more significant than ourselves, and all of us become worthy of the title "servant of Hashem."

"*Mekimi mei'afar dal, mei'ashpos yarim evyon* (*ibid.* v. 7), He raises the needy from the dust, from the trash heaps He lifts the destitute." The verse does not mean that this is something Hashem does occasionally. It is His constant occupation. We are never to despair, because the theme "the stone the builders despised has become the cornerstone" is in all the stories of *Tanach*; and even today, "whatever one's personal situation may be, there is no person who does not see many wonders and acts of Divine kindness in his life" (*Mesillas Yesharim* Chapter 8).

"*B'tzeis Yisrael miMitzraim* (*Psalms* 114:1), When Israel went out of Egypt, the house of Jacob from a people of alien language, then Judah became His sanctuary, and Israel His dominions." Each language is a unique mode of expression, affecting the way we look at life (e.g., someone who "*davens*" is not quite the same as someone who "prays," and "Tatty," "Daddy" or "Abba" is light-years away from "my old man"). For our ancestors to achieve their goals, it was not enough to be free from bondage, but they also had to leave the people of alien language, alien culture and a worldview at odds with our mission.

So too with us. Besides the obvious need to distance ourselves from the harmful influence of bad friends, we should know that even good friends do not always understand our aspirations, and we must find friends and mentors with whom we share a common spiritual language. It is no accident that Hashem arranged His world with Ashkenazim and Sephardim, misnagdim, chassidim and dozens of subgroups, each with its own worldview and dialect. Although most of our spiritual challenges come within ourselves and are independent of our surroundings, a change of *shul* or school or mentor or friend can also make a difference, and it sometimes makes sense to cautiously seek them out.

"*Lamah yomru hagoyim ayeh na Elokeihem* (ibid. 115:2), Why should the nations say, 'Where is their G-d now?'" "The word *na* always denotes a plea" (see *Rashi* to *Exodus* 11:2), so that we could translate this verse, "Why should the nations say, '*Please*, where is their G-d?'" There is holiness in human beings, even in nations who oppress us. Anti-Semites who go out of their way to attack us, missionaries who exert all their efforts to convert us, do so because they recognize that Jews are unique, without knowing precisely what that uniqueness is. Their rage stems from their souls' understanding that Israel is the teacher but they have not yet learned their lesson, and therefore even their insults (like a child's plea for attention expressed as a verbal attack on the parent) are compliments in disguise, asking, "Please, where is their G-d, so that we may share Him too?"

"*Yevarech yirei Hashem, haketanim im hagedolim* (*Psalms* 115:13), He will bless those who fear Hashem, the small as well as the great." Fear of Hashem, not mere fear of punishment but to feel the awe of Hashem's Presence Itself, is among the highest spiritual attainments, and among the most difficult (*Mesillas Yesharim* Chapter 24). Even so, there are different levels of spirituality, and if we cannot become one of the "great" *yirei Hashem*, we can still try to be among the "small."

The Gemara uses an expression, *bar bei rav d'chad yuma;* "a yeshivah student for one day" a year is also considered somewhat a yeshivah student. If we set aside just a few minutes a day to try to live on a higher plane, in speech and deed and conscious awareness of the presence of Hashem; small as the effort is, it is enough to place us in a select group, worthy of His special blessing and aid.

"*Ahavti ki yishma Hashem es koli tachanunai* (*Psalms* 116:1), I love when Hashem listens to my voice, my supplications." Who does not love it when Hashem hears his prayer? But it means: Even when Hashem does *not* give me what I ask for, the honor and closeness of Hashem listening to me when I speak and His wanting to hear what I have to say, that alone fills me with feelings of love (Rav *Simcha Zissel Ziv*). If the President of the United States gave you a private audience, you would remember it and speak about it forever, even if you did not vote for him. How much happier we should be that, whatever our troubles, we are always invited to a private audience with the One Who listens, and truly helps.

"*Mah ashiv laHashem...*(ibid. v.12), How can I repay Hashem for all His kindness to me? I will raise the cup of salvation and call out in the Name of Hashem. I will pay my vows to Hashem in the presence of His entire people." King David's way of trying to repay Hashem is to thank Him *publicly*, to "call out" and to express gratitude in the presence of the entire people. Every Jewish celebration, from a wedding to a Shabbos or Yom Tov meal, is a public expression of thanks. On these occasions we should take the opportunity to verbalize our gratitude to Hashem, to count our blessings in the hearing of family and friends, and to thereby strengthen the impression these celebrations make upon us.

"*Hallelu es Hashem kol goyim...ki gavar aleinu chasdo* (ibid. 117:1), All nations, give unrestrained praise to Hashem... for His kindness has overwhelmed us." Why should the nations praise Hashem for His kindness to us? One answer is that we Jews know only a small fraction of the plots that have been hatched against us, and the many miracles Hashem made to save us. But the nations, who know the full scope of their attempts to do us harm, and who know how often their plans were frustrated by Divine intervention, *they* can give special praise to the greatness of Hashem, and they will do so in the days of Redemption to come.

"*Hodu laHashem ki tov, ki l'olam chasdo* (ibid. 118:1), Thank Hashem for He is good, for His kindness is forever." How do we know that even a miserable life is worth living? One answer is that no matter how difficult your circumstances may be, at the arrival of Yom Tov your mitzvah is to say the *berachah* of *Shehechiyanu*, "Blessed are You, Hashem...Who

has kept us alive and sustained us, and brought us to this day."
We say Hallel no matter what our personal circumstances or
mood may be, because "Hashem's kindness is forever," always, whether we see it or not and whether we think He loves
us or not. As the saying goes, even if you don't believe in Him,
He continues to believe in you.

"*Zeh ha'shaar laHashem* (ibid. v. 20), This is the gate to
Hashem." What does the word "This" refer to? Rav Simcha
Zissel Ziv wrote that it refers to the verse two lines earlier,
"*Yasor yisrani* (ibid. v. 18), G-d has chastened me exceedingly." All of us, without exception, have our share of
hardships (some receive a greater share), because hardship
is a necessary prerequisite to refinement of the soul. The righteous stand out in their understanding of this truth and in their
being able to use it, which gives them serenity in this world
and an honored place in the Next: "*This* is the gate to Hashem,
the righteous will enter through it."

"*Odcha ki anisani* (ibid. v. 21), I thank you for You have answered me and You became my salvation." Rav Simcha Zissel
translated it, "I thank You for You have inflicted *suffering*
("*anisani*" from the word *inui*), and You became my salvation."
Midrash Rabbah (*Exodus* 21) tells of a king traveling on the
road who heard the cry of a princess attacked by highwaymen. The king rescued her, received her heartfelt thanks, and
they went their separate ways. The king was seeking a wife,
but when he made overtures to the princess he was rebuffed.
What did the king do? He waited until the princess traveled
again, and then he *hired* the same highwaymen to attack her
again, so that he, the gallant king, could charge in on his white
horse to rescue her yet another time.

When we are troubled we cry out to Hashem and await His
answer, and from our perspective it is the trouble that leads
to our outcry. But the truth is the exact opposite, that Hashem
often creates the trouble for the sole purpose of encouraging
us to cry out! The crying out leads to a closeness, which when
followed by deliverance makes us closer still. It is an ongoing

process throughout life, and we give thanks for it as part of our Hallel.

"*Ana Hashem hoshiah na, Ana Hashem hatzlichah na* (*Psalms* 118:25), Please Hashem, save us! Please Hashem, give us success!*" Praying for success immediately after praying for salvation sounds a bit incongruous, like a gravely ill hospital patient pleading with Hashem for a speedy recovery and also to strike it rich in the stock market at the same time. But in doing so we express our confidence in Hashem's power, that the troubles are only a means of bringing us closer to Him, and it is only reasonable that the closeness of salvation should bring the closeness of prosperity in its wake. It is also our way of saying that, just as we pray in time of trouble, we will continue to offer prayers in times of success, seeing it all as coming from the same Source.

"*Kel Hashem vayaer lanu, isru chag ba'avosim ad karnos hamizbeiach* (ibid v. 27), Hashem is G-d, and He gave us light, bind the Festival offering with cords until the corners of the Altar." This is also the Scriptural source for *Isru Chag*, that one should have some celebration even on the day after Yom Tov (*Shulchan Aruch Orach Chaim* 429).

The connection between *Isru Chag* and the plain meaning of the verse is: Hashem's salvation is not an experience to be lived through and then forgotten. It should give light to our path in life, and we should feel the urge to do something concrete to express our new insight: "He gave us light," therefore bring an offering to thank Him. In the same way, the light of Yom Tov should not be extinguished when we bid Yom Tov farewell. We should seek to take something with us, and this thought is expressed by whatever small celebration we have on *Isru Chag*, a symbol that the light of Yom Tov will continue to guide our path.

THE FOUR ANSWERS

When *Rambam* (Maimonides) formulated his famous Thirteen Fundamental Principles of Faith, he elicited a great deal of criticism; because the Torah is so vast and such a unity, that everything in it can be considered fundamental, and it is beyond human ability to define the Torah in terms of categories or general principles. Nevertheless, we all need to fashion what the Midrash calls *oznayim l'Torah*, to get "a handle on the Torah"; to seek out ways to sum up Torah ideology to help us grab hold of it, and bring it fully into our lives.

But if we are seeking to discover an authenic, universally accepted definition of Jewishness, we need look no further than the beginning of the Pesach Haggadah. Pesach is the night when we explain to our children why we are Jewish, why we observe the mitzvos of the Torah and what the meaning of that observance is. Since most people read the Haggadah's explanation of Judaism without ever realizing that this is what it is, let's review it together, point by point.

The child sees all the preparations that went into making Pesach, and all the mitzvos of the *seder*, and the child asks the four questions of "*Mah nishtanah.*" We do not ask analogous questions on Shavuos or Succos, because our intent at the *seder* is not merely to explain the significance of this night, but to explain the significance of *every* night, and every day, the meaning of every mitzvah we do. And at the *seder*, we answer the four questions with four answers (strange how most of us have never counted the answers, but the number does not appear to be four):

Answer #1. "*Avadim hayinu l'Pharoah b'Mitzraim*, we were slaves to Pharaoh in Egypt, and Hashem our Lord took us out with a mighty hand and outstretched arm," meaning, with miracles and with demonstration of His love.

Answer #2. "*V'ilu lo hotzi Hakadosh Baruch Hu es avoseinu*, if Hashem had not taken our ancestors out of Egypt, then we and our children and children's children would still be slaves to Pharaoh," even today.

Answer #3. "*V'afilu kulanu chachamim, kulanu nevonim*, and even if all of us are wise and understanding and learned in Torah, we are still obligated to relate the story of the Exodus from Egypt."

Answer #4. "*V'chol hamarbeh l'saper biyetzias Mitzraim harei zeh m'shubach*, and the more one tells about the story of the Exodus from Egypt, that person is to be praised"; as in the example given by the Haggadah of Rabbi Eliezer and his colleagues who spent the night discussing the Redemption, until dawn.

Four answers, or possibly four points which are part of a single answer. Since this is the only time of year the Torah commands us to do this, it means that these answers are intended to give the children a basis for understanding their Judaism throughout the year. What is the meaning of these four points?

Point #1. "We were slaves, and Hashem took us out." There are very many pathways which lead a person to commit himself or herself to the Torah. But the way suggested by the Torah tradition itself is to be inspired by a sense of gratitude: Hashem took us out. He saved us. And we keep His mitzvos because it is the least we can do to say thanks.

You can fulfill a mitzvah in order to get something out of it, reward in Heaven or a good feeling here on earth; but though such motives are not wrong, they have the weakness of being purely self-centered. The ideal is that our mitzvos should express a unique relationship: Hashem, You have done so much for me, I want to show appreciation by doing something in return.

Point #2. "If Hashem had not taken our ancestors out of Egypt, then we and our children and children's children would still be slaves to Pharaoh." Literally. Because the principle is: The Torah is *not* ancient history, it is all relevant to me and my family, right now. This is because nothing in this world happens by chance, and if Hashem had not willed it so, there would not have been an Avraham or a Moshe to save us. Had Hashem not taken us out of Egypt, we would be there enslaved even today.

The corollary of this principle is that we are required to feel a joyous appreciation not only for today's blessings, but also for the blessings of yesterday, and the day before. Were you happy on the day you became a *bar-* or *bas-mitzvah*? The day you received your driver's license or the day of your wedding? Well then, if you are still married and you still know how to drive, and you are still over the age of *bar-* or *bas-mitzvah*, then you should be deliriously happy with the combined joy of all those blessings you possess. But we grow accustomed to our blessings, and we forget them, and therefore on Pesach we tell our children and ourselves: Never forget. It is not the past. Enjoy your blessings, because they are with you, here and now.

Point #3. "Even if all of us are wise and understanding and learned in Torah, we are still obligated to relate the story." There are many Jews who say, "I'm not observant, but I'm a good Jew at heart." That is like the fellow who insists that he loves his wife, but he just never talks to her. Any relationship that is real must be lived, and expressed in words and deeds. Even if a year ago you told your wife and children how much you love them, this year you have to say it again, and hopefully more than once a year.

This is what we say at the *seder*: Yiddishkeit is an ongoing relationship with Hashem, and the bonding process continues with each new mitzvah, and with each new repetition of the old formula for saying: We're together, and we are one.

And Point #4. "The more one tells about the story of the Exodus, that person is to be praised." What is the Haggadah telling us that we do not already know? Certainly, more words of Torah and more mitzvos are always praiseworthy!

The commentaries explain: The Haggadah brings its proof from Rabbi Eliezer, who spent the entire night at the *seder*. But later the Haggadah says that the mitzvah of telling the story is in effect only during the time when there is a mitzvah to eat the *korban Pesach*, the Passover lamb, and Rabbi Eliezer's opinion in the Gemara is that we must finish eating the Passover lamb before midnight. It thus follows that after midnight there was no longer any mitzvah for Rabbi Eliezer to discuss the Exodus, so why did he stay up till dawn?

The answer is, and the principle of Judaism is: A relationship in which each partner does only what they are obligated to do, and nothing more, is hardly a relationship at all. If a married couple comes to the Rabbi to ask, "What is the minimum we are required to do for each other according to *halachah*?" it means that the marriage is already on the verge of breaking up.

And at the *seder* we tell our children how Rabbi Eliezer stayed up relating details of the Exodus until dawn, to teach them, and ourselves, that part of Torah law is to do *more* than the law; not to seek out every leniency and loophole, and not to pat ourselves on the back when what we need is a swift kick in the pants.

This is why, when a guest leaves your home, it is a mitzvah to accompany him at least a few steps. Inside your home, perhaps you extended hospitality because politeness compelled you to do so, and as soon as the visitor leaves you slam the door with a sigh of relief. But when you accompany your guest, when you go the extra mile to show that you enjoyed his company and are not in a hurry to be rid of him, that makes an impact on the character of the entire visit (Rav Simcha Zissel Ziv of Kelm). The same is true in general, that the measure of our Jewish character is not only what we do, but also our willingness to do more than is required, because we are proud to have the opportunity to do it.

So the Pesach *seder* gives us a four-point program, a way to *live* the Torah: to firmly establish our commitment on a bedrock of gratitude; to realize that the blessings of the past are very much with us in the present; to express our sacred feelings again and again, in word and deed; and to demonstrate a desire to do more than the minimum, happily.

Thinking about these ideas while enjoying our Yom Tov meals will transform our Pesach. And if we review the Haggadah, we will find in the section of Maggid, the retelling of the Pesach story, something astonishing: Maggid ends with a repetition of these same four principles, in exactly the same order! Maggid ends with the *berachah* we recite immediately before drinking the second of the four cups. We say:

"*Baruch atah Hashem...asher g'alanu v'ga'al es avoseinu*, THANK YOU, Hashem, for redeeming us and our ancestors." There is the principle of gratitude.

"*V'higianu halaylah hazeh*, and thank You for enabling us to reach THIS night." The blessing and joy are not just the past, but we give thanks for this night, the blessing that is here right now.

"*Le'echol bo matzah umaror*, this night, to eat matzah and maror." We say we are happy to express our gratitude in AC-TIONS, actual mitzvah deeds.

"*Kein Hashem Elokeinu, yagiyenu l'moadim ul'regalim acherim*, please Hashem, give us the opportunity to celebrate additional Yomim Tovim," MORE mitzvos in the future, because we want to do more, with joy; "*s'meichim b'vinyan irecha*, happy in the building of Jerusalem and rejoicing in Your Service" in the House of Hashem, speedily in our days.

THE SANDWICH CONTROVERSY

The Haggadah mentions a *machlokes*, a difference of opinion between Hillel and the other *Chachamim* (Sages), whether on Pesach night we are to eat matzah and the bitter herbs of *maror* separately, or together in a sandwich. To be on the safe side, we do it both ways.

This appears to be a straightforward question of halachah, a legal issue with no special lesson to teach us at the *seder*. However, *Sefer Maggid Meisharim* (quoted by Rav Moshe Shternbuch) teaches that we place the bitter *maror* on top of the matzah, because the bitterness of Egyptian bondage preceded the Divine redemption. Even before we try to understand what this means, we see that eating matzah and *maror* together or separately, in addition to being a question of Torah law, also contains an element of commemorative symbolism. Clearly it involves some idea we are meant to reflect on at the *seder*. Let's examine what that idea might be.

We know that *maror* is intended to remind us of the bitterness of slavery. Matzah serves to remind us that Hashem is in complete control, and Divine salvation arrives in the blink of an eye. One minute, we were enslaved to Egypt; the next minute, Hashem took us out so quickly that there was not even time to bake a loaf of bread. *Maror* symbolizes bitterness and matzah, redemption. On Pesach we must remember both aspects, but the Rabbis disagreed as to how it should be done.

The *Chachamim*, Hillel's colleagues, ruled that matzah and *maror* are to be eaten separately. The intense pain of Egyptian slavery, and the overwhelming joy of Divine redemption, are conflicting emotions. Pesach night we must relive both, but we cannot be expected to feel both experiences at the same time. Hillel disagreed, and put matzah and *maror* together, because his understanding of the Torah is that we must simultaneously re-create both the bitterness and the joy, that each emotion should help us to comprehend the full dimensions of the other.

But how is it possible to experience the true pain and the true joy, vicariously, at the same time? The answer is *zecher l'mikdash k'Hillel*; this combination is a *mitzvah d'oraisa* (Biblical commandment) only when we also had the *Beis Hamikdash* (Holy Temple) and we ate, along with matzah and *maror*, *korban Pesach*, the Pesach lamb.

The simple meaning of the *korban Pesach* is to symbolize that "the Lord is my shepherd." But *Sefer Hachinuch* adds that the lamb is also a reminder that Hashem chose us to become a *mamleches kohanim*, a term which Rashi translates as "a kingdom of nobles," of princes. We Jews are to feel that we have been entrusted with a mission which elevates us, not in order to look down on others, but in order to live a higher life, suffused with an aristocratic idealism.

To represent this idea, the Pesach lamb must be eaten indoors, and no bone may be broken, and we are not to leave any leftovers; because princes do not eat outdoors on the steps, and they do not need to break bones to suck out every dot of marrow, and princes don't have to eat leftovers.

With the *korban Pesach*, if you feel ennobled by the honor of being Hashem's ambassador to the world, *then* you can eat matzah and *maror* together; then you are elevated enough to come to comprehend how bitterness is a necessary step to attaining joy, and how slavery was required to bring us to fully appreciate what Divine liberation meant.

In the midst of personal suffering, it is very difficult to perceive how the bitter *maror* leads to redemption. But the Pesach lamb raises us above our personal hardship, it elevates us to a sense of noble calling in our lives; and with the elevated, bird's-eye view we can see the big picture, how all that occurs is part of Hashem's Plan.

Today, we no longer have the *Beis Hamikdash* and the Pesach lamb, and we do not have the spiritual elevation which enabled us to view bitterness and joy in perspective. And therefore today, even Hillel agrees that the Biblical mitzvah requires us to eat matzah and *maror separately*. But in addition to that mitzvah we also eat the sandwich, in order to remember that it *is* possible for a Jew to understand, and to come to see the Hand of Hashem in all things; to know that whatever our difficulties may be, Hashem is still here, still taking care; and to know that underneath all the *maror*, the matzah of Redemption lies waiting, to arrive in its designated time.

Today we are not literal slaves, but Pesach remains for us the time for personal Redemption. We say in the Haggadah, "*Avadim hayinu l'Pharaoh b'Mitzraim*, we were slaves to Pharaoh in Egypt". We also say, "*Mitchilah ovdei avodah zarah hayu avoseinu*, originally, our ancestors were idol-worshippers," our father Avraham's father, Terach, was in the retail idol business. What is Avraham's idol-worshipping father doing in the Haggadah?

The *Sefer Oheiv Yisrael* answers: One of the lessons of Pesach is to never give up hope, no matter how insurmountable the problem appears to be. Do you suffer from the burden of a wicked Pharaoh? Do not give up. Hashem saved us once, and He can surely do so again. Or do you suffer from the burden of your own emotions? Are you enslaved by fears or desires or thoughts that rip you apart, thoughts that you are far from the Torah and will never be close to Hashem? Do not give up. You cannot be worse than Terach, Avraham's father who worshipped idols, and who was willing to kill his own son because of it.

In the end, even Terach was redeemed, by having Avraham as his son; and the Midrash says that eventually Terach himself did *teshuvah*, he also came to know Hashem. And we say this in the Haggadah to teach us that all kinds of personal Redemption are possible, physical, emotional, spiritual; whatever the prison, even one of our own construction, if we do not cease to wait for Hashem, He can always set us free. And therefore we still eat matzah and *maror* together, reminding ourselves that Hashem can make every sort of bitterness a prelude to Redemption, and that the *Beis Hamikdash* will someday return, to elevate us all to the nobility of joy.

FREE FOR WHAT?

The central mitzvah of the Pesach *seder* is to relate the story of the Exodus from Egypt, especially to tell it to the children. However, the parents of *yeshivah ketanah* or Jewish day school children often find it difficult to perform this mitzvah, because the children are busy telling what *they* know, and they sometimes know more than the parents. Even among children who have only a very limited Torah education, if they know enough to ask the four questions, they have almost certainly learned the basic answer. So what is this special mitzvah for the adult to retell?

It is striking that this mitzvah, as commanded in the Torah, is not expressed as a mitzvah to teach, or to inform. In the *Shema Yisrael*, where we are commanded to teach our children Torah in general, it says *velimadtem*, teach them. When the Torah commands us to teach our children of Hashem's Revelation at Mt. Sinai, it says *vehodata*, inform them, make them know. But on Pesach night the mitzvah is simply *vehigadta*, tell it over, an emphasis on our telling rather than the child's listening. Why is this so?

Near the beginning (but not at the *very* beginning) of the *seder*, we proclaim, "All who are hungry, let them come and eat." It is a generous invitation. But who will hear it, when we say those words in the privacy of our own homes? Whoever we invited to the *seder* is already there, and our meal has already begun, with *Kiddush*; so why is this said now?

It is also odd that we make this announcement only on Pesach night. *Rambam* (Maimonides) writes that we are obligated to invite poor people at every Yom Tov, so why is this said only at the *seder*?

Pesach is a time for families to come together, and my *Rebbeim* (Torah teachers and mentors) always urged everyone who is able to make their Pesach at home. But in ancient times, almost every Jew *did* go away for Pesach. They went up to Jerusalem.

In Jerusalem, the mitzvah was to eat the *korban Pesach*, to finish an entire Pesach lamb at one sitting. A whole lamb was too much for one family, so Jews would combine in large groups, dozens of people crowded together in one house, and it was not necessarily a family feast. Why does the Torah desire that Pesach be celebrated this way?

One more question, one of the most famous of questions: How did Jews through centuries of oppression, enslaved in ghettos and prisons and labor camps, manage to celebrate Pesach liberation? The haggadah itself says that we are not fully free today, "*Hashata avdei*, Now we are slaves." So what is the meaning of the freedom we celebrate *seder* night?

To sum up, there are four questions: (1) Why is the Pesach story a mitzvah to tell over or relate, rather than a mitzvah to teach? (2) Why make a generous invitation to the poor at a time and place they cannot hear us to be able to accept? (3) Why does the Torah want the Pesach lamb to be eaten in large groups? And (4) what is the meaning of freedom for Jews who are still in chains?

The answer is:

Slaves are not free to choose what to do with their lives. But slaves can be liberated, and still have no freedom, if there are still no meaningful choices available for them to make. It is not uncommon for people who retire from their jobs to die soon after, because they have nothing to do with their days and they feel their lives are without meaning. Mothers whose children grow up and leave home may find themselves suffering from Empty Nest Syndrome, no longer needed by anyone. Teenagers who have too much freedom and too little responsibility often end up getting into real trouble.

As a philosopher once put it, the most deprived kind of person is the man whose life has no purpose. If life is truly meaningless, and if the only joy is the existential thrill of the moment, then drugs, sadism and every terrible crime become entirely *reasonable*. Whatever it is, do it for kicks. Or even if there is no reason at all to do it, do it anyway, because, why not?

Those of us who lived through the late 1950s and early 1960s may find it difficult to recall the starry-eyed enthusiasm with which the world watched one African nation after another become freed from British or French colonial rule. Independence, *Uhuru* (that's Swahili, not Aramaic)! Freedom! But democracy quickly became dictatorship, and many hundreds of thousands of innocents continue to be slaughtered by nations who do not know how to use the freedom they possess.

And therefore, we begin preparing for the Festival of Freedom a month in advance, on Purim, when we give the *machatzis hashekel*. The original *machatzis hashekel* was a coin given by every Jew to the *Beis Hamikdash* (Holy Temple) just before the month of Nissan. Once Nissan began, all the coins *together* were used to purchase *korbanos*, offerings brought on behalf of the entire Jewish people. A single coin by itself was not enough money to purchase an offering, but each Jew was not allowed to contribute more than one.

This was a public demonstration: Being a member of *Klal Yisrael* means that you are part of a people, a nation, with a national purpose to perpetuate the will of Hashem on earth. All individual contributions are of equal value, and no single contribution is sufficient by itself. We *need* one another, and all of us have our purpose in whatever we contribute to Hashem and to His people. That is how we prepare for the month of Nissan, and for Pesach.

The Torah's mitzvah required a large group to come together to eat the Pesach lamb, and the group had to officially *count* each individual as a participating member, in advance. That too was a public statement: We need you as part of the group, and you count. Even the most learned, pious and wealthy people had to ask others to join them, because we all need other people to be able to fulfill our obligations, as one.

When we proclaim, "All who are hungry come and eat," that is *not* an invitation. The guest at your *seder* was invited long before (surely before *Kiddush!*). But our announcement means: Thank you for coming; thank you, because you give me the mitzvah of hosting you, and because of you, I am needed.

Kol dichfin concludes with the words "*Hashata avdei*, Now we are slaves," which appears to be an abrupt change of subject. But the connection is: Even if we are enslaved, we still celebrate that Hashem's liberating us gave us our national mission, which endures; and if I can invite you to share what little I have, then that is an element of freedom which is reason enough to celebrate, and to await the Redemption to come.

The mitzvah of relating the story is not intended to provide information to the children. They know it already from school, or they remember it from last year. The mitzvah to tell the story is for *me*, the *teller*. It is to remind me that *I* am a link in the chain, that I am the torchbearer, and it is I who have the honor to pass it on. Our ancestors who left Egypt with Moshe Rabbeinu have a message for the children of the 21st century, and the person who was chosen to deliver that message is me.

Will the children listen? We pray that they will. But even if, Heaven forbid, some of them do not, our mission remains unchanged. Our ancestors did not always listen to the prophets either. But in the Book of *Isaiah* (6:8), Hashem asked, "Who can I send, and who will go out for us?" and the prophet answered, "Here I am, send *me*."

Before Pesach it is a venerable custom that every Jew contributes to *maos chittim*, charity to provide for the Pesach needs of the poor. It is possible that in ancient times, Pesach was not much more expensive than other Yamim Tovim. But Pesach is when I affirm that I am part of this nation and the nation needs me; I am responsible for all of them, and must do what I can; hence, *maos chittim*.

And therefore Pesach is a time to try to strengthen our sense of purpose, the feeling of belonging to a people with a mission. It is a good time to read biographies of great *tzaddikim*, *our tzaddikim*. It is also a time when different families practice their individual *minhagim*, different customs which are reminders that each of us has something special to contribute.

And Pesach is therefore also a time to ask: What additional contribution can *I* make to further the national mission of which I am a part? Is there some new mitzvah or area of Torah learning or *davening* or *tzedakah* activity which it is time for me to accept? The more we take part, the more we come to feel that this Torah is our own, and that *we* went out of Egypt, all generations together; and together we await the day when Hashem will bring all of us back to the *Beis Hamikdash*, to celebrate together once again.

ALL NATURAL, NO ADDITIVES

Two recipes are used in virtually all Kosher-for-Pesach Matzah sold in the United States today: (1) flour and water, used for "regular" matzah; and (2) flour, eggs and apple juice, used for "egg matzah." General Ashkenazi Jewish practice is to permit consumption of egg matzah only by children or people in poor health (consult your rabbi for details). But even people in poor health may not use egg matzah to fulfill the mitzvah of matzah at the *seder*, because "mitzvah matzos" must be made with at least some water (because they are required to have had the *potential* to become true chametz during the baking process, and this requires water), and egg matzah is made without any water at all.

Matzah with flour, juice *and* water is not made today, due to several halachic concerns. If, however, we had such matzah, we are still not to use it for the *seder*, because such matzah, called *matzah ashirah* ("rich" matzah) does not ful-

---

(Halachic discussion in the first part of this chapter is based on Mishnas Yaavetz Orach Chaim #16, by Rav Betzalel Zolti of Jerusalem.)

fill the Torah's requirement of "*lechem oni*," "poor man's bread" or "the bread of affliction." For *lechem oni*, we require matzah made from only flour and water.

A question: If someone used this *matzah ashirah* for the *seder* (out of ignorance, or no other was available), does he fulfill the mitzvah of eating matzah? The simple answer is, of course not! *Seder* matzah must be *lechem oni*, and eating other matzah is no mitzvah at all. This is indeed the opinion of the *Magen Avraham.*

However, *Maharal of Prague* disagrees. *Maharal's* opinion is that *seder* matzah includes two separate mitzvos: "*B'erev tochlu matzos*, on Pesach evening eat matzos"; and "*lechem oni*, bread of affliction." One who used *matzah ashirah* for the *seder* did not fulfill the second mitzvah of "bread of affliction," but he *did* fulfill the first mitzvah of "eat matzos." (For more details see *Mishnas Yaavetz*, who writes that *Rambam's* ruling is like that of *Maharal.*)

As noted above, we do not have this matzah today, so this question is unlikely to have practical applications for us. But the controversy over the essential nature of *seder* matzah — must it be *lechem oni* by definition, or is *lechem oni* an additional, separate mitzvah — those two opinions are relevant to our whole understanding of the mitzvah itself, as we will see.

It is not necessary to know a reason for most mitzvos, other than that they are Hashem's command. But as we say in the Haggadah, understanding the "why" of matzah is part of the mitzvah itself ("*Matzah zu*, this matzah that we eat, ror what is it?" and "whoever did not say, i.e. explain, these three things has not fulfilled his obligation").

The simple explanation is that matzah is a reminder of how quickly Redemption came. One moment we were slaves, but the next moment we left Egypt in such haste that we had no time to bake a loaf of bread; "the salvation of Hashem comes in the blink of an eye," and so remains our hope even today.

According to this explanation, matzah represents *cheirus*, freedom, which is why we recline when we eat matzah, in the manner of the freeman. But there is a problem: If matzah symbolizes freedom, why is it *lechem oni*, the bread of affliction?

How we resolve this paradox will depend on how we view the mitzvah of *lechem oni*. If *lechem oni* is an inseparable aspect of mitzvah matzah, an essential part of *defining* what mitzvah matzah is (the *Magen Avraham's* position), then the "bread of affliction" remembrance must somehow be an integral part of the *cheirus* remembrance, so that "freedom" without "affliction" is not freedom at all. If, however, *lechem oni* is an additional mitzvah in the matzah (as per *Maharal*), we could then say that matzah represents *cheirus* while *lechem oni* stands for some other, additional lesson.

Rav Shamshon Raphael Hirsch takes the first view, that the "bread of affliction" symbol is a necessary part of the *cheirus*, freedom symbol, in the following way: The message of Pesach is not that we were set free, but that *Hashem* set us free. Freedom itself can lead to arrogance, and in becoming our own masters we can forget the Master of All.

Matzah is the type of bread eaten by slaves, and it was not what our ancestors planned for the menu on their first day of freedom! But Hashem arranged it that they left in such haste that they ended up eating matzah, to teach the lesson: We are free only by command of Hashem and for the purpose of serving Hashem, for without Him we would still be enslaved, eating the "bread of affliction." Matzah symbolizes *cheirus*, but a *cheirus* that is only from Him, for His sake.

According to Rav Hirsch, the "affliction" aspect is vital to correctly experiencing the aspect of "freedom" without arrogance, and it is therefore self-evident that matzah which is not *lechem oni* is not mitzvah matzah at all, as in the view of the *Magen Avraham*. But in *Maharal's* view that *lechem oni* is an *additional* mitzvah, not part of the lesson of freedom, what is the lesson of "bread of affliction"? We could answer that *lechem oni* is to remind us of slavery, but the bitter *maror* does that already; and in any case, it would be strange for the Torah to tack on remembrances of slavery in the very symbol of freedom (matzah), if the two are not intertwined as per Rav Hirsch.

On the second day of Pesach we begin counting the *Omer*, counting 49 days to the day Hashem gave us His Torah, on Shavuos. One reason for counting is to remember that our Pesach liberation was intended for a specific purpose, that Hashem did not shake Heaven and earth to make us free merely to allow us to sleep late on Sunday mornings. Pesach freedom was to enable us to go to Mt. Sinai, to accept the greatness of the Torah.

In line with this idea, Rav Simcha Zissel Ziv said: One reason why the Torah wants matzah to be *lechem oni*, poor man's bread without extra additives, is to teach us: If you seek greatness in Torah, if you hope to achieve something in matters of the spirit, then you cannot focus your attention on egg matzah, or matzah with jelly and jam, or Passover chocolates.

Please don't misunderstand me. Matzah with jam or jelly is one of Hashem's many blessings to us, as is PC (Passover chocolate, of course). But if chocolate is *important* to us, if material pleasure and possessions are priority items, the other priorities like Torah, *davening* and character will inevitably be pushed down into second (or third or fourth) place.

Studies of superstars in the world of business show a common denominator, that none of them worked only 40 hours a week. Fifty– or 60–hour workweeks or even more were not uncommon; because they had a vision of what they wanted, and they pursued that vision with a single-minded intensity that allowed nothing to stand in their way.

On Pesach, when we relive the beginning of our careers as Jews, the Torah says: Start with the bare necessity; plain matzah, no additives; to remind yourselves that you cannot allow petty material things to stand in the way of what is truly important in your life.

You may recall the story of Anne Scheiber, who passed away a few years ago. Anne Scheiber was a low-level government employee who spent her life saving and investing her money, in order to be able to give it to charity. She had a goal and a vision, to accomplish something worthwhile, and when she passed away she left an estate of *$20 million* for Jewish education.

Anne Scheiber's achievement is an inspiration of heroic proportions. But the way her story was written up in the general media was so bizarre, that it provides an object lesson in how *not* to look at life. National weekly newsmagazines noted disapprovingly that "she always wore the same cheap coat and hat." They reported that, oddly, she did not buy new furniture. Astonishingly, for years, she did not even own a color television set. And horror of horrors, instead of subscribing to the *Wall Street Journal*, she would read the newspaper in her local library!

The media tried to psychoanalyze her, to determine what led to such strange behavior. She was a child of the depression. She was alone, she was fearful, she was this or she was that. *Nebach*, our society is so *meshugah* that it does not even comprehend how someone else can be sane.

There is no compelling reason to buy new furniture, if the old will serve. If you can read the stock prices in the library, there is no mitzvah to subscribe to the *Wall Street Journal*. And living without a color TV set is *mutar lechol hadeios*, all the authorities permit it. But people immersed in pettiness cannot comprehend that someone else would choose to live simply; not because she was depriving herself, but because she had a higher priority, a goal she achieved whose effects will be felt for generations.

Pesach is the time when we hand down the Tradition, to children and grandchildren and each one of us to the other. Pesach is also the time to ask ourselves, what is the essence of that Tradition we hope to hand down? Once you shake off all the *charoses* from the matzah, if you get down to bedrock, what *is* most important to you to pass on to the next generation? Or, to put it another way, if *chas v'shalom* you were to die tonight, what would you like people to say about you at your funeral tomorrow?

On the last day of Pesach, we pledge *tzedakah* at *Yizkor*, remembering those who are gone; and demonstrating that their influence lives on, in that they inspire us to want to give *tzedakah* in their memory. It is a good time to think about what sort of influence we ourselves would like to have, and how *we* wish to be remembered.

And as we thoughtfully chew on our matzah, with or without jelly, it's a good time to think about getting back to basics: to want to live in such a way to be remembered as a person of Torah learning and mitzvos and kindness, all natural, without additives; to inspire our families that the link between Pesach matzah and Shavuos Torah is a bond that will remain forever, in our homes and hearts.

BUT WHY MUST IT BE SO EXPENSIVE?

A famous question: At the Pesach *seder* we celebrate our freedom. We also recall the slavery by eating matzah, which the Torah calls "*lechem ani,* poor man's bread." Isn't it strange, then, that to celebrate freedom, we have to slave for many days and weeks in preparing and cleaning and *kashering* and cooking and shlepping? And is it not downright bizarre that *shemurah matzah*, the poor man's bread, costs a super-expensive umpteen dollars per pound? (I would have written the actual price, but I was afraid it might be much higher by the time you read this.)

Perhaps life was simpler in the olden days, and Pesach was cheaper. But there was always cleaning and *kashering*, and the trip to Jerusalem to eat the *korban Pesach*, the Pesach lamb, was for many people a major expense. Clearly, this expenditure of treasure and toil is somehow part of the Divine plan. What does it accomplish? And why did Hashem arrange it this way for Pesach more than for any other Yom Tov?

Pesach is also unique in that at the *seder*, we symbolically re-enact the historical event the Yom Tov commemorates. We eat poor man's bread and bitter herbs, and saltwater to recall the tears, and *charoses* to remember clay used in bricks. By contrast, on Shavuos, the day the Torah was given at Sinai, we do nothing of the sort, not even an assembly at the foot of a mountain in the Catskills. We do sit in a *succah* on Succos to remember how Hashem took care of our ancestors in the Wilderness, but there is no Succos *seder* to recall the details. Why only on Pesach?

We all know certain ideas and feelings which are important truths, but whose meaning we cannot readily articulate to be able to explain to others. Love for one's child or one's spouse, for instance, to make great sacrifice for another person and to do it with joy, can we truly explain this to people who have never experienced it themselves? Or to take the example of patriotism, love of country; in several parts of Africa loyalty is solely to one's tribe, and the idea of allegiance to a nation is utterly alien. Democracy, free speech, individual worth, so many principles that Americans take for granted are unknown in other cultures, and they are exceedingly difficult to teach if the student has no feeling for them to begin with.

The difficulty one experiences in explaining various ideas does not make them any less real. But not every reality can be adequately conveyed by mere words. To grasp the true essence of some things, the what and the why, you must experience them yourself; there is no other way.

The classic *Sefer Hachinuch* lists and explains the 613 mitzvos of the Torah. In describing the mitzvos of the Pesach *seder*, he writes (Mitzvah #16). "My son, do not object and ask: 'Why did Hashem command so many mitzvos to remember this miracle (of the Exodus)? Would not one remembrance be enough to place the thing in our minds and keep it from being forgotten by our children?' Your objection in this does not stem from wisdom.

"Because, my son ... know that a human being is shaped by his own actions, and his feelings and all his thoughts are continually drawn after the deeds he does, for good or for bad. Even a totally wicked person ... if he will constantly occupy himself in Torah study and mitzvah observance, even if his motivation is not for the sake of Heaven, he will be turned towards the Good ... for the hearts follows the deeds ... For this reason the Sages said, 'G-d wanted to give merit to Israel, and therefore He gave them an abundance of Torah and mitzvos.'"

This passage is one of the most famous in all Rabbinic literature. "*Ha'adam nifal lefi pe'ulosav*, a human being is shaped by his own actions." Some people assume that *Sefer Hachinuch* is referring to the supernatural spiritual power of mitzvos, that holy deeds affect the human soul and character, as do sins. This is certainly true, but *Sefer Hachinuch* makes no explicit mention of the spiritual aspect. Rather, his approach in this passage appears to be psychological; that in general, our thoughts and feelings can be changed by modifying our behavior.

Torah ideas do not need to pass the test of any modern psychological theory; quite the reverse. But it is worthy of note that this principle of *Sefer Hachinuch* is echoed in contemporary research.

Scientific studies have been conducted comparing two different methods of attempting to influence other people's opinion. One method selected was verbal, to have the subject of the experiment read books and attend lectures which argued the merits of a particular viewpoint in a clear and logical manner. The second method tested was role-playing, having the subject himself pretend to be a spokesman for the particular point of view. The second technique was found to be far more effective. People who take on the role — even only pretending — of advocating a belief are in the end more likely to come to accept the belief than others who only listen or read about if passively.

Every mitzvah is a building block in the structure of the Torah, and in general it is not for us to say that one mitzvah is more important than another. But Pesach in one way is unique, because the Pesach *seder* comes to answer the question, Why? Not only "*Mah nishtanah*, Why is this night different," but also "*Mah ha'avodah hazos lachem*, What does this service mean to you?" Why do we keep the Torah, why are we Jewish, why are we loyal to Hashem not only at the *seder* but throughout our lives? Pesach is when we pass on the *Mesorah*, the Tradition, to the next generation; a tradition not only of stories and facts, but of fire, to convey the white-hot core of Yiddishkeit, body and soul.

We can transmit Torah information in classrooms, in lecture and books, and we do. But for the child to feel the "why" of Torah, a flaming love for Torah, an understanding that goes beyond mere words, just as love itself is beyond mere words — to transmit *that*, we use not *sefarim* (books), but role-playing. *We* went out of Egypt, *we* eat the poor man's bread, and bitter herbs and saltwater with tears, and *we* recline with the wine of freedom. We act it all out, because that is the very best way to come to understand that Judaism is not just acting.

Going a bit deeper: When Rav Yisrael Salanter started the Mussar movement in Lithuania in the 1840s, he would travel from town to town spreading his message of the need for a comprehensive program of developing character, spiritual growth and fear of Hashem. It was the custom in those days for *maggidim* (traveling preachers) to "pass the hat" after their *drashos* (Torah lectures), but Rav Yisrael at first refused to do it, so as not to detract from the dignity of his Torah ideas. However, he soon realized that this was the wrong approach and he acceded to the old custom, because when people *pay* to hear words of Torah, they value them more, and the message sinks in more deeply.

In general, the more you work for something, the more you come to appreciate it, which is why a parent's love for a child is usually stronger than the child's love for the parent. To use the words of psychologist Dr. Roger Brown: "If action cannot be adequately accounted for by factors other than a favorable judgment, then there is a need to *make* the judgment favorable in order to justify the motivations for what has been done ... (In general,) the poorer the excuse for an action, the greater the need to make it rational by means of attitude change."

That means: If Pesach is merely an excuse for an annual family dinner, that can justify the expenditure of a few hours and a few dollars. But if I am going to spend many hundreds of dollars, and hundreds of hours of hard work, I must have a good reason for it; and therefore, inside my head, I begin to develop more feeling for how important Pesach is. If it is not important, why am I doing all this? By doing it all, I persuade myself how important it all is to me.

Of course (and this is important), we are not speaking about deceiving ourselves with beliefs that are untrue. Also, if someone is resentful to begin with, their negative attitude may well push them further away from the Torah. But for observant Jews who have a positive, healthy attitude to begin with, all the effort and all the expense strengthen in their minds the importance of what Pesach means to them. The Gemara says that pain of childbirth contributes to the mother's love for her child; in the same way, the challenges of Pesach preparation (not necessarily painful) teach us that the chain of tradition is ours to treasure, forever.

The Haggadah tells us, "*Rasha, mah hu omeir,* The wicked son, what does he say?" A great Chassidic teacher once made a play on words, and read: "*Rasha, mah hu?,* What is it that will make a son wicked?" The answer is "*omeir,*" "saying," what he heard his parents saying as he grew up. If he heard them saying, "*Oy,* Pesach, it's so hard, and so expensive," then he learns the lesson that Yiddishkeit is a burden to be thrown off at the earliest opportunity. On the other hand, "*Chacham, mah hu,*" what produces a wise son?" Also "*omeir,*" what *his* parents say: "*Baruch Hashem,* another chance to be able to make Pesach."

Planning a wedding is hard work, and very expensive; but families do it happily, because they know it is the creation of a whole new relationship, to last forever, *b'ezras Hashem* (with Hashem's help). Pesach is not quite as expensive, though most people make Pesach more often than they make weddings. But Pesach too is the creation of a relationship; and it has the potential to produce a similar *simchah*, to share a bond with children and grandchildren, and memories of sacred joy to last forever, *b'ezras Hashem.*

HASTE MAKES ...
PESACH

Most Jews who have had even minimal Torah education can answer the question, "Why do we eat matzah on Pesach?" But relatively few know the precise answer that is given in the Torah itself. In *Parshas Re'eh* (*Deuteronomy* 16:3): "Do not eat with it (the Pesach lamb) any *chametz*. Seven days you will eat matzos, the bread of affliction, because you left Egypt in haste; in order that you will remember the day of your leaving the land of Egypt all the days of your life."

Note that matzah does not commemorate only liberation — liberation is not even mentioned here — but it is to recall the *haste*, the rush in which we left.

What was the rush? Rashi's commentary explains: "The haste was not yours, but Egypt's, as it says, 'And Egypt pressed the people, to hasten to send them out'" (*Exodus* 12:33). The Egyptians pressed us to leave before they all died from the plague.

This is something new, or at least something most of us have never thought about, which is the same thing. The Torah is saying that the essential point of matzah, more than freedom, and more than miracles, is that it is to remember Egypt's *haste*. And this is something to remember "all the days of your life." Why is this haste the most important thing to remember?

In the Friday night Kiddush, we proclaim that Shabbos is *zecher liyetzias Mitzraim*, Shabbos is a remembrance of the Exodus from Egypt. How is Shabbos connected with the Exodus?

Shabbos is the reminder that the world has a Creator. But it is theoretically possible for someone to believe in a Creator Who made the universe, and then ceased to concern Himself with it. Perhaps the Almighty wound up the cosmic clock and then retired to Florida; just as most people today believe in G-d, but the G-d they believe in this not very much a part of their daily lives. (Author's note to readers under the age of 30: In your grandparents' day clocks were wound by hand, hence the expression, "wound up the cosmic clock.")

The Exodus teaches us: The *Creator* of the Universe is also the *Controller* of the Universe. The Master of all takes an interest in all; and, as the Exodus demonstrates, He even makes miracles, that's how much He cares and guides our lives. Pesach gives life to Shabbos, because the Exodus shows that the Creator is still involved, pulling the strings from above the stage so that His Will be done.

However, the question now becomes: Granted that we need Pesach to testify that the Creator of the Shabbos is still actively involved, but once we have Pesach, why do we need the Shabbos? Once the Exodus from Egypt demonstrates that Hashem is in complete control, why require a weekly reminder that He is also the Creator? The first of the Ten Commandments is "I am Hashem your G-d Who took you out of the land of Egypt." Once we recognize the G-d of the Ten Plagues and the splitting of the Red Sea, Hashem who controls everything, what is the importance of the Fourth Commandment reminding us that He also *made* everything?

Every year on Pesach, usually on Shabbos *Chol HaMoed*, we read *Shir HaShirim*, the Song of Solomon or Song of Songs, an allegorical poem depicting the love between Hashem and the people of Israel. The plain meaning of the verses, the allegorical "plot," tells of a king who fell in love with a shepherd girl. As an absolute monarch, he had the power to make her his bride by force. Even so, he did not have the power to compel her to change her attitude to love him. Some things are beyond the power of even the mightiest kings.

Without going into the deeper meaning of *Shir HaShirim*, we can come to see that this limit on the king's power is a serious *mis*perception we have in our relationship with the King of Kings. If a loyal Jew with firm *emunah* (faith) has a serious problem, he is likely to think: "Yes, Hashem can help, but he cannot make my wife love me." Or a Jew seeking employment says, "Yes, of course Hashem can help me find a job — but there are no jobs to be found." Or, "I do have faith that Hashem could help me meet a marriage partner, if I lived in Jerusalem or Brooklyn. But since I am stuck here in Yehupitzville, even Hashem does not make something out of nothing!"

But that attitude is selling Hashem short. Pesach teaches us that Hashem actively *controls*. Once we know that He controls, then *Shabbos* tells us: If the necessary raw materials are absent, He *creates*. Hashem not only directs the flow, but He makes the flow; and if all solutions to your problem are unworkable, He can make a new solution out of nothing.

Perhaps the most open miracle of this generation was the implosion of the Soviet empire in the late 1980s and early 1990s; and what makes this miracle so open is that absolutely no one dreamed of it. Communism was triumphant, winning one country after another. Freedom in Eastern Europe, emigration for Soviet Jews, or yeshivos in Moscow and Kiev? Laughably impossible. But "He Who sits in Heaven laughs"

(*Psalms* 2:4) the last laugh, and at a word from Hashem, the world turned upside down.

You may have read about the Jewish young man from New York who went to study in a Buddhist monastery in Thailand, surely lost to us forever. But in the monastery, the monk in charge turned out to be *another* Jewish young man from New York, and he told *this* young man he should go to learn in a yeshivah, and he did! Hashem's reach is infinite. And on Pesach we eat matzah to recall not only that He liberated us, but to recall how the same Pharaoh who had said, "Never," Pharaoh who had warned Moshe, "Do not come to see me again," it was that same Pharaoh who ended up running through the streets yelling, "Where is Moshe? Moshe, Aharon, leave, go, just as you said, and bless be me too."

Matzah symbolizes *chipazon*, haste, such haste that we had no time to bake a loaf of bread. *Chipazon shel mi*, Whose haste? *Shel Mitzraim*, That of the Egyptians, the ones who swore they would not let us go; it was *they* who hastened to comply with the word of Hashem. Hashem, the Creator and the Controller, not only freed us, but He transformed the Egyptian will.

And the Torah commands us to remember this all the days of our lives; to know that Hashem, Who can create a whole new attitude in Pharaoh to make him ask *us* for a blessing, He can surely change the attitudes of our employers and neighbors and relatives, and whatever other situation *we* think is beyond repair.

In *Eretz Yisrael*, for many years there have been *Gedolei Torah*, outstanding Torah leaders, who have taken public positions on important religious and political issues of the day. But surprisingly, some of the most outspoken rabbis, who never hesitated to speak their minds, never articulated (at least not publicly) a position on what Israel should do concerning its problems with its Arab neighbors.

I once heard a suggestion that perhaps these Sages themselves do not know what to do, because there *is* no alternative that makes good sense. Some problems simply have no solutions. But at the same time, the Sages know that where no solution exists, Hashem can always create a new one; and if we seek to do His Will, He will show us that He is not bound by the restrictions of *realpolitik*.

We must surely do everything we can to deal with problems, as best we know how. But we must always keep in mind that Hashem has His own methods, and He can transform enemies into friends; swords into plowshares; and Jews into holy people, people who live with the memory of the miracles of the liberation from Egypt, *kol yemei chayecha*, each day, all the days, of your lives.

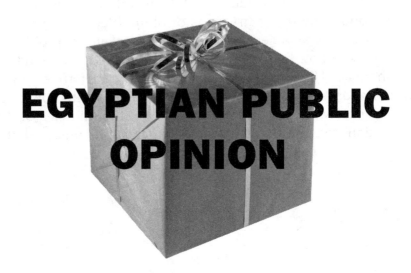

EGYPTIAN PUBLIC OPINION

The purpose of the miracles in Egypt, the Ten Plagues and the splitting of the Red Sea, was not only to give us our freedom. Hashem could have achieved that goal simply by arranging for a democratic Abraham Lincoln-type Pharaoh to inherit the Egyptian throne, which would have been less complicated and much more cost-effective. But the Torah says that the reason for the miracles was, "and Egypt shall know I am Hashem" (*Exodus* 7:5); "that you (Pharaoh) shall know there is none like Hashem" (ibid. 8:6); "that you (Pharaoh) shall know that I am Hashem in the midst of the land" (ibid. 8:18); the plagues were to teach Pharaoh and the Egyptians that Hashem is in control.

Why the great effort to teach the Egyptians, who were not interested and who did not really learn the lesson anyway, at least not until their "crash course" at the Red Sea? And why does Hashem speak of teaching Egypt so much more than He mentions teaching Israel? A number of different answers have been given to this question, but one that allows us to begin with a good story is the following:

An Eastern European *maskil*, a Jewish writer who had abandoned mitzvah observance, once came to a prominent Rav and said: "Rebbi, it's the 19th century! Humanity has made so much progress, we have come so far since the old days at Mt. Sinai, we don't need all the laws of the Torah anymore." The Rav replied: "You remind me of a story, about the inhabitants of the village of Chelm."

(Author's note: One of our readers objected that making Chelmites the butt of jokes should be *lashon hara*, forbidden gossip, since Chelm was the name of a real town. In this story, however, all Chelmites are fictitious. Any resemblance to people in your *shul* or *beis medrash* is purely coincidental.)

"The good people of Chelm," the Rav began, "wished to expand their village, but they were blocked by a mountain which stood just outside the city limits. The villagers assembled for a brainstorming session, and the mayor of the town came up with a plan: If all the villagers worked together, their combined strength could *push* the mountain away and open up space for expansion. The ingenious suggestion was unanimously approved, and early the next morning several hundred able-bodied Chelmites marched to the mountain and began to push.

"It was a warm spring day, and all the men removed their jackets and placed them in a large pile behind them. An hour later, a gang of thieves passed by, and when nobody was looking they stole all the jackets and ran off. When it was time for the workers to go home, and they wondered if they had been successful, the mayor said: 'Good people, see how far we've come! We have made such progress that we cannot even see the pile of our jackets!'"

And the Rav concluded: "My friend, the same holds true for you. Mt. Sinai stands eternal, it can't be pushed away. But the 'clothing' of Judaism — the sense of dignity, of style, of pride in mitzvos, of honor to be one of Hashem's people — you have let all the beautiful 'clothes' be stolen from you. And now that it's missing, you think you have made progress!"

The biggest roadblock on the path of the American Jew is not that he lacks faith or interest. It's that he lacks a sense of pride; pride in belonging to the people of the Torah, pride in belonging to the people who gave the world the moral foundation upon which it stands.

This is not a new problem. Even in ancient times, when our ancestors were tempted by idol-worship, you will find that they never invented an idol of their own. It was always the temptation of the *non-Jewish neighbor's idol*, the god of Egypt or Moab or Canaan, always a feeling that whatever the gentiles respect, we have to have it too.

How did idolatry finally come to an end among Jews? The last great trial was the idol of King Nevuchadnezzar of Babylon. Three Jewish heroes, Chananiah, Mishael and Azariah, refused to worship it, and they were thrown into a fire; but Hashem made one of the last great obvious miracles, and everyone saw the angel of Hashem sent to rescue them. At that point, the Gemara says, the *pagans* turned to the Jews and said: "You Jews have a G-d like this, and *you* worshipped idols?" As the Gemara puts it, the pagans covered the Jews with spit, in their scorn for Jews who could be so lacking in self-respect to act like — pagans. And that ended our centuries-old infatuation with idolatry.

The same sociological-religious problem, and the same solution, existed for the people of Israel in ancient Egypt. After the ninth plague, the Torah tells us: "The man Moshe was very great ... in the eyes of Pharaoh's servants, and in the eyes of the people" (*Exodus* 11:3). "The eyes of the people" — which people? The Egyptians? No, the Jews (*Ramban*).

Earlier, the Jews were saying, "May Hashem judge you" and punish you. But now that they had seen the miracles, and now that Moshe *was very great in the eyes of Pharaoh's servants*, now the Jews respected him too.

The chief purpose of the miracles in Egypt was not to teach the Egyptians, but to teach *our* people the great meaning of life. But we had been slaves for so long, so many years of suffering under Egyptian physical domination *and* cultural domination (cultural, not in the sense of art and music, but in one's whole outlook on life and society), that it was enormously difficult to change ingrained patterns of thinking. So Hashem's method of instruction was, "I will make the gentiles know that I am Hashem"; and that way, the Jews will learn it as well.

We say in the Haggadah, *"Hashata avdei,* Now we are slaves." Even today we are enslaved intellectually and emotionally by our need to fit in, to slavishly imitate whatever style or fad or pseudo-intellectual trend is this week's fashion among our non-Jewish neighbors; and we forget that *we* are to be the role models for the world to follow, not the other way around.

Rav Meir Leibush Malbim was Rabbi of Bucharest, Romania, at a time when many of the community's wealthiest Jews had cast aside mitzvah observance in order to be more like their non-Jewish neighbors. It happened that one of these men was called to the Torah for an *aliyah* in *shul,* and he recited the *berachah,* "Blessed are You, Hashem ... Who chose us from all the nations and gave us His Torah," with loud enthusiasm, as if he were a *tzaddik.* The Malbim said: "Certainly he thanks Hashem for giving *us* the Torah, for this way he can imitate the *goyim* by doing nothing; but if Hashem had given Torah to the *goyim,* this man in his wish to imitate them would have to keep all 613 mitzvos!"

Pesach is a time to remember — and to teach our children — that when our nation was born, even Egypt recognized that we are a special people, with a unique mission on earth. Non-Jews still recognize this today, from the stone-throwing street urchin to philosopher Eric Hoffer, who wrote extensively of the mystery of the Jew ("Jews think they are the same as other people, but they are not"). Fairly or unfairly, Jews are treated differently in the media, the courts and the United Nations, because the world knows there is something special about the Jewish people, without knowing what it is.

And Hashem arranged all this, even to make miracles, so that *we* should remember: We *are* special, with a special job to do. And the first step to doing our job is to recover our stolen "clothing," the pride in who we are and what we represent, and what we have to offer to all the world.

THIS NIGHT, AND EVERY DAY

Most of the mitzvos we fulfill at the Pesach *seder* are *mi'divrei Sofrim*, of Rabbinic origin. Two special *seder* mitzvos are *min haTorah*, written in the Torah itself. One is "*ba'erev tochlu matzos*, on this evening you shall eat matzos." The second is "*vehigadta levincha*, and you shall tell your son" what Hashem did for you, the story of *yetzias Mitzraim* (the Exodus from Egypt), how Hashem liberated us from Egypt.

As special as this second mitzvah is, at the *seder* we make a point of mentioning that the *mitzvah* is not restricted to Pesach; that, in a sense, the *seder mitzvah* is not so special after all. We begin by asking, "Why is this night different from all the nights?" And we answer that this night is intended to thank Hashem for saving us. Then we quote from the Torah (*Exodus* 16:3), "*lemaan tizkor*, that you shall remember the day of the Exodus all the days of your life," and we take note of the Gemara's comment that we are obligated to mention the Exodus daily (and possibly nightly) throughout the year; which we indeed do, when we recite the last verse in the three paragraphs of *Shema Yisrael*.

But if the mitzvah to speak of the Exodus is every day, and possibly every night, we are now back to our original question: "*Mah nishtanah*, Why is THIS night different?" What is special about our mitzvah at the *seder*?

To this question great rabbis have answered that for the daily mitzvah of mentioning the Exodus one line in the *Shema* is sufficient, but on Pesach night our mitzvah is to elaborate, to tell the story in detail. Another difference is that one may recite the daily *Shema* most anywhere, alone or in company, while the Pesach story requires parent and child to come together to tell the story over matzah and *maror*.

But this answer leads to yet another question, which is: Why are we commanded to make mention of our deliverance from Egypt in two different ways? If the "bread of affliction" and bitter herbs and *seder* pageantry are important to make the point, why not do them every day? When we read daily in the *Shema*, "*Ani Hashem Elokeichem asher hotzeisi eschem mei'Eretz Mitzraim*, I am Hashem your G-d Who took you out of the land of Egypt," why do we not at least hold a pinch of horseradish and inhale, to help us remember?

The answer must be that one can remember perfectly well without the tangible symbols. But if symbols are unnecessary, why on Pesach night are we commanded to tell the story specifically over matzah and *maror*, and four cups of wine? If you wish to answer that the Torah did not desire to make our daily mitzvah too difficult, then halachic sources should at least mention the symbols as a *hiddur*, an optional extra enhancement to hold matzah and *maror* (instead of *tzitzis*) at the *Shema* throughout the year; but we do not find this in the sources.

Perhaps the explanation is: To become inspired, the nature of human beings is that we need excitement, and we need experiences which are out of the ordinary. We tend to listen to visiting guest speakers more attentively than to speakers we hear regularly. Dramatic plays have more powerful emotional impact than well-reasoned essays. We therefore need an annual *seder*, an exciting evening (two evenings, outside of *Eretz Yisrael* where we need more), to inspire us with the enthusiasm of reliving the Exodus from Egypt.

But it is also part of the human condition that life is not meant to be lived on a continuous high of excitement. A philosopher once wrote that part of a child's education should be to learn to get used to boredom. The mind cannot develop properly if it is flooded with an endless stream of nerve-tingling stimuli. Today's American child comes home from school, looks around at the television, radio, stereo, VCR, games and toys, shelves of books, and says, "There's nothing to do!" And the result is the stunting of growth of the child as an autonomous thinking, feeling human being.

A veteran teacher criticized children's television, even educational television, for making children so used to high-speed entertainment that many of them can no longer sit absorbed in a book, or enjoy human teachers who are incapable of transforming their shape and color the way cartoon characters do. In the Jewish towns of Eastern Europe, one reason for the universal interest in Gemara study was that Gemara never had to compete with professional comedians and cable TV. Too much mental sugar, even if it is healthful sugar (and all the more so if it is not), prevents the development of a sensitive intellectual palate.

What is true of the mind is also true of the emotions, that there is a limit to how long the heartstrings can be intensely pulled. How many young couples marry in a burst of romantic fever, only to discover soon after that marriage's reality is so very different from the dream? It is not that Romance is doomed to die. It is that a healthy long-term relationship must have an everyday quality to it, a pleasant routine part of your day and your life rather than an endless series of episodes of thrilling adventure.

The Gemara says that *chassidim harishonim*, the saintly men of earlier generations, spent a whole hour reciting the *Shemonah Esrei* prayer. After prayers, they would spend yet another hour in the synagogue before leaving. Rav Yaakov Moshe Lessin, *Neishtater Rav* (Lithuania), explained the necessity for the extra hour:

Rambam (Maimonides) writes that the prayers of these holy people elevated them to levels akin to prophecy. But if one goes from the prophetic state directly to the mundane, if one descends rapidly from the sublime to Manhattan (or even Brooklyn), the change is so drastic that one feels no way to connect the awesome *kedushah* (sanctity) with one's daily routine, and all the inspiration gets lost. This happens to many of us after Yom Kippur, when the contrast between the holiness of Yom Kippur and the workaday world is so great that we feel we can take nothing with us, and the personal elevation of the holy day quickly dissipates.

The *chassidim harishonim* would therefore remain in the synagogue after prayers, just as people who exercise set aside a period to cool down after exercising is over. They would ask themselves, What did I get from this *Shemonah Esrei*? What was the inspiration, or the insight? How can I translate that lofty mood, or the profound lesson, into simpler form, some practical application I can use in my work or at home?

Pesach night, properly utilized, is a night of unique inspiration. We outside of *Eretz Yisrael* are blessed with two nights of Yom Tov, enabling us to make up on the second night for areas where we fell short on the first, like runners who take time to hit their stride. At our *seder*, besides hearing what the children learned in school, and besides perusing *Haggadah* commentaries for insights ingenious and profound, we should also take a quiet moment just to say "thank You" to Hashem. Thanks that we are alive; thanks that we and our families are not enslaved; thanks that we are not living in a war zone, or in a country that denies us freedom to keep the Torah; thanks that we have family and friends with whom to share a *seder*; and thanks that we have what to eat, even at inflated Passover prices.

And then we should take that emotion of thanks, and the emotions of love and joy, and try to translate them, to encapsulate them all in a feeling of simple contentment, a quietly pleasant image in your mind that brings a touch of a smile to your face. As you, seated at the *seder* table together with those you love, chew your *afikoman*, and together with all the generations back to Moshe and Aharon, try to compress 3,000 years of Pesach experience into a simple "thank You, Hashem"; so that some taste of the spirit of matzah remains in your mouth, at *seder's* end.

And then, when we recite the *Shema*, the next day, and every day, we should briefly call to mind that pleasant mental image of contentment. And we should leave the daily *davening* not with excitement, not with the rousing singing of *Chad Gadya* and not with the thrill of finding the *afikoman*; but with an extra bit of quiet happiness knowing that we are indeed blessed to be alive and free, to have families and friends, and to be together as one people, united in our goal of becoming the people of Hashem.

THE TWO JEWISH CALENDARS

The names of the months in the secular calendar are derived largely from Greek and Roman mythology, and for that reason some Jews prefer to always write a number for the month instead of a name, e.g. to write 1/22 for January 22 (the Europeans write it 22/1). However, the Chasam Sofer was opposed to this because it contradicts an explicit statement of the Torah, "*Hachodesh hazeh lachem rosh chadashim, rishon hu lachem lechadshei hashanah*, This month (of Nissan) will be for you the head of months, it is first for you of the months of the year" (*Exodus* 12:2). So for us, Nissan is #1, not January.

Whether it is in fact forbidden to write number "1" for January is a halachic issue outside the scope of this chapter. But we need to understand: If Nissan is our first month, why does every Jewish calendar begin in Tishrei? The Torah itself states that the Day of *Teruah*, Rosh Hashanah, the start of the new year, is on the first day of the *seventh* month. Does the year begin in Tishrei, or Nissan?

Adam Harishon, Adam, the first human being, fashioned directly by the Hand of Hashem, possessed a level of sanctity far beyond our ability to comprehend. The Midrash says that angels confused him with his Creator and wished to sing divine praises to him, and that even his heels (i.e., the lowest part of the body) were radiant like the sun. But Adam was not a Jew, and he did not possess the even higher level of holiness of the 613 mitzvos; and therefore when we say the daily morning *berachah* of "*shelo asani goy*, thank You, Hashem, for not making me a non-Jew," we mean even a non-Jew like Adam (the Slabodka Mashgiach, in *Torah Avraham*).

The *kedushas Yisrael*, the sanctity of the people of Israel, is unique. But that sanctity does not *replace* the sanctity of being a human being, it *adds* to it. The 613 mitzvos are the advanced course of obligations we accepted at Sinai, in *addition* to all the original obligations we had as human beings created *b'tzelem Elokim*, in the image of Hashem (*Toras Avraham*). Rabbi Shamshon Raphael Hirsch expressed this idea by describing the Jew as "Mensch-Yisrael"; or, as Rav Avigdor Miller put it, acting correctly as a Jew is to build a second story on top of the ground floor of acting correctly as a human being, and some people try to build a second story without ever constructing the first (heard by the author).

And therefore, because of who we are, we reckon the year in two different ways: As human beings, we count from Rosh Hashanah, the anniversary of the creation of Adam and Eve. As members of *Klal Yisrael*, we count from Nissan, the anniversary of the founding of the Jewish nation.

Everything in the Torah is intended to teach us something, and there are surely lessons to be learned from the two Jewish calendars.

Sefer Hachinuch gives a reason for the Torah's mitzvah of "*v'samachta b'chagecha*," rejoicing on Yom Tov, as follows: "For a human being is made in such a way that his nature requires that he rejoice from time to time, just as he requires food and rest and sleep; and the Lord wished to give merit to us, His nation and His flock, and He commanded us to make the celebration for His sake ... He established for us festival times during the year to remember the miracles and kindnesses He did for us; and in those times He commended us to care for the body with the rejoicing it requires ..."

This is a new idea, to say that Yom Tov, in addition to its intrinsic sanctity and commemorative aspect, also comes to meet our specific emotional needs. The *shalosh regalim*, the three pilgrimage festivals of Pesach, Shavuos and Succos, are considered a three-part series; and we can suggest that each of these Yamim Tovim, in addition to its *kedushah* and its commemoration, also comes to show us how to deal with one of three fundamental human needs.

Of all human needs, the most basic is physical security. Not to know where your next meal is coming from, to be homeless or in danger, makes it next to impossible to focus one's mind on anything else (compare *Rambam, Dei'os* 4:1, "for it is impossible to understand or know anything of knowledge of the Creator, if he is ill"). And therefore it is perfectly understandable that the first Yom Tov of the year — counting from Tishrei — is Succos, to recall how Hashem protected us and provided for our every need in the Wilderness, and that He continues to do so today.

After basic physical needs are taken care of, there comes a desire for a sense of identity and self-esteem, a yearning to be somebody and belong somewhere. It is a crushing burden to see yourself as completely alone, cut off from society with no place to fit in. This is one reason why people marry, and why they root for football teams and political parties, because we need other people to provide us with a frame of reference by which to define ourselves.

And this is why the second Yom Tov, counting from Tishrei, is Pesach, which recalls how Hashem chose us to be His special people, each of us part of a nation with a history and destiny. The Exodus from Egypt took place before the giving of the Torah, which perhaps explains why even Jews who know nothing of Torah still feel inside that being Jewish makes us different, somehow. And if Jews forget, there are always non-Jews who remind us; because even non-Jews sense the truth that Jews are a distinct, separate people, the separate people we became, on Pesach.

Finally, if you possess material security and sense of identity, a third great human need is for a sense of purpose, direction in life, a reason to get up in the morning. In the words of the French philosopher Jean Paul Sartre, "The fundamental existential question is, Why *shouldn't* I commit suicide?" That is one reason why people work at jobs and raise children and march for various causes, to feel that they are needed, and that there is a purpose to their lives.

And this is why the third Yom Tov from Tishrei is Shavuos, the day we received our all-encompassing purpose in life; the day we were assigned our sacred mission of sanctifying the universe, by receiving and living the Torah.

So we now have a cycle of Yamim Tovim, Succos, Pesach and Shavuos, teaching us the lessons of security, identity and purpose, all in their natural, human order. However, in this natural order, there is the danger that a human being may never fully move on from Step One to Step Two. You begin with security and from there proceed to discover your sense of identity and purpose. But what if the search for identity and purpose itself begins to threaten your material comfort?

What happens if you discover the Shabbos, but it comes into conflict with your present occupation? If you are already well established in your business or profession, will it be so easy to redefine your identity, to say, "I am not a physician or a store owner, but I'm a Jew who happens to make a living and tries to serve Hashem in my capacity as a physician, store owner," etc. If my starting point and foundation has been material security, will I now be able to accept the goal of Torah and view my livelihood as merely a stepping stone to reach spiritual success?

Along comes the Torah to reply: "*Hachodesh hazeh lachem*"; for *you*, the people of Israel, count Nissan as the first month. In halachah, the cycle of Yamim Tovim is not

Succos/Pesach/Shavuos. Instead, Pesach comes *first*. Before all else, I'm a Jew. And, no matter what we hope our children will *accomplish* in life, good Jews are what we hope for our children to *be*.

Once identity is established, we then seek our sense of purpose, which is the Torah, on Shavuos. I may not have much in the way of Torah learning or doing, just as some people don't have very much money. But people without money do not stop trying to get some, and the most spiritually impoverished person can still view Torah and mitzvos as the great goal for which to strive.

Finally, after attaining a sense of identity and purpose, once we possess our Jewishness and our Torah; only then, *after* Pesach and Shavuos, comes Succos, the Yom Tov focusing on our material blessings of sustenance and security. Once you know who you are as a Jew, and after you have your clear spiritual goal, *then* you can focus on material things to see them as gifts from Hashem. Then, you can pursue your occupation and accumulate possessions, because after Pesach and Shavuos you will be able to put occupation and possessions into perspective, seeing them as the means to a noble end.

It is not easy to put material things in second place. Perhaps that is why the Torah says, "*Hachodesh hazeh LACHEM*," for *you*, the Jewish people, Nissan and Pesach come first. For other nations it is too much to ask. But getting our priorities straight is easier when we realize that, in the end, it is only the person rich in spiritual possessions who can fully enjoy the material possessions he or she.

Emperor Napoleon, for instance, had the greatest power, riches and honor of any man on earth in his day; and looking back in his later years, Napoleon said: "I have had only six happy days in my life." On the other hand, Rav Yisrael Salanter lived in poverty and experienced major disappointments all his life; but Rav Yoizel Horvitz of Novardok said: "I have known only one happy man in my life, and that was Rav Yisrael Salanter."

On the Shabbos before *Rosh Chodesh* we pray (in *Birchas Hachodesh*) that all Israel should be blessed with *osher u'chavod*, wealth and honor; so we hope that by the end of the Yom Tov cycle every Jew should be able to afford a mansion of a *succah*, with the finest furniture to fill it. But we also hope that every Jew will first come to experience the riches of Pesach and Shavuos, to know who we are and where we're going, to be able to enjoy the destination, when we arrive.

SKETCH FROM AFAR: THE MAN BORN ON PESACH

You may be familiar with the well-known phrase in the introduction to the ethical classic *Mesillas Yesharim*, that "some of the most well-known truths are also the most overlooked." This holds true also for certain human beings: Some of the most famous people are seldom thought about seriously, and as a result we do not realize how little we really know of them. As an example, take Yitzchak Avinu, the Patriarch Isaac, son of Avraham.

Everyone knows Yitzchak Avinu, of course. Anyone who's been to Hebrew school, and lots of people who haven't, have heard of Abraham, Isaac and Jacob. Those who have learned Gemara and Midrash know that "the *Avos* (Patriarchs) are the Divine Chariot," and "Avraham, Yitzchak and Yaakov are considered *shekulim zeh kazeh*, all of equal value" (*Bereishis Rabbah*).

Since everyone knows, ask the next Jew you meet, "In what famous story in *Chumash* is Yitzchak Avinu the hero or main character?"

"Main character? That's too easy. Everyone knows the answer is *Akeidas Yitzchak*, the Binding of Isaac, where our father Avraham showed his willingness to sacrifice his son, and Hashem promised Avraham: 'Because you did this thing, and you did not hold back your son, your only one, I will bless you, and I will make your seed like the stars of the heavens,' etc."

See the problem? The hero of the *Akeidah* is clearly our father Avraham, not Yitzchak. Yitzchak seems a passive, secondary figure throughout.

(The reason Avraham is the hero is that "the Lord tested *Avraham*" — *Genesis* 22:1 — by asking him to sacrifice Yitzchak, an act which contradicted Hashem's promise that Yitzchak would be the father of the Jewish people, and which also contradicted everything Avraham had ever learned and taught about Hashem's kindness until now. This required Avraham to take all he knew and everything he stood for, and surrender it to the Will of Hashem. Yitzchak's test, difficult as it was, was not quite as hard; Yitzchak's test was to be willing to surrender his own life, a test which many of his descendants through the centuries have also faced and passed.)

"All right, then, if Yitzchak was not the main character in the *Akeidah*, what about the story of the *berachos* (blessings), when Yitzchak Avinu wanted to bless Eisav (Esau) and Yaakov came and took the *berachos* instead?"

Once again, Yitzchak Avinu appears mainly in a supporting role. The main character is our father Yaakov; and Yitzchak is portrayed in an unflattering light as a father tricked for years by his wicked son Eisav, and now tricked, albeit for his own good, by his righteous son Yaakov. We will try to explain Yitzchak's actions later on. But for now, where does the Torah tell a story in which Yitzchak clearly occupies center stage, and where we see why he merits to be one of the *Avos*?

"Wait, I have it! In *Parshas Toldos*, we are told that Yitzchak Avinu went to the land of the Philistines as a result of a famine (just as his father Avraham had done). For protection, he pretended that his wife was his sister (as Avraham had done). He had a run-in with King Avimelech when the king discovered the truth (just like Avraham), and he had a problem with the Philistines stealing his wells (ditto). Yitzchak Avinu is clearly the main character here (though it's odd how much of the story repeats Avraham's), and the Torah says how Hashem blessed him ... But acts of outstanding greatness, where the Torah says or shows why Yitzchak is one of the *Avos*, from *Chumash* itself it isn't clear ..."

But aside from the Midrash quoted above that the three *Avos* are *shekulim*, equal, we find that, in at least one area, Yitzchak is *superior* to Avraham and Yaakov; and this area is the one which, for us, is perhaps the most important of all. In *Mesechta Shabbos 89b*:

"In the future, *Hakadosh Baruch Hu* will say to Avraham, 'Your children have sinned to Me!' He will reply, 'Master of the world, let them be blotted out for the sanctity of Your Name.'

"Hashem will then say, 'I will speak to Yaakov, who went through the travails of child-rearing, perhaps he will plead for mercy for them.' He will say to him (Hashem to Yaakov), 'Your children have sinned!' He will reply, 'Master of the world, let them be blotted out for the sanctity of Your Name.'

"Hashem will say, 'The elders have no understanding, and the children have no counsel.' He will then say to Yitzchak, 'Your children have sinned to Me!' He will reply, 'Master of the world, are they my children and not Your children? At the time that they said to You *Naaseh* before *Nishma* ("Whatever Hashem has said, we will do and we will listen," accepting the Torah on faith even without knowing the content), You called them "My firstborn" (*Exodus* 4:22), and now they are *my* children and not *Your* children?'"

(Yitzchak Avinu continues in our defense, and then the Gemara concludes:) "The Jewish people will say: 'For *you* are our father, for Avraham did not know us, and Yisrael (Yaakov) did not acknowledge us'" (*Isaiah* 63:16).

Yitzchak is not just one of the Fathers. Yitzchak is the one who merits to be called *our* Father, above the rest. But the Gemara does not explain why only Yitzchak comes to our defense, and it remains yet another mystery about one of our most well-known men, who is also one of our most overlooked.

It is clear from the Gemara (*Mesechta Rosh Hashanah* 10b) that the time of year when the three *Avos* were born was pre-arranged by Hashem as part of His overall Plan. I would have thought it more appropriate for Yitzchak Avinu to be born at Rosh Hashanah time; the *shofar* recalls the ram offered in Yitzchak's place, and in *Shemonah Esrei* we pray, "and the binding of Yitzchak, may You mercifully remember to his descendants this day." Pesach, when we commemorate the founding of the Jewish nation, would have been a good birthday-time either for Avraham, the first Jew, or for Yaakov, father of the Twelve Tribes of Israel. But the truth is otherwise.

The Gemara in *Rosh Hashanah* (ibid.) says that according to Rabbi Eliezer, our Fathers Avraham and Yaakov were born in the month of Tishrei, while Yitzchak was born on Pesach. Rabbi Yehoshua differs, and is of the opinion that all three *Avos* were born in the month of Nissan, but he agrees that only Yitzchak was born on Pesach.

To make sure we get the point, *Midrash Rabbah* tells us that Yitzchak was born Pesach time, "*moed tzeischa miMitzrayim*, the time of your going out from Egypt" (*Genesis* 53). The Midrash (*Shemos Rabbah* 15) adds that *Akeidas Yitzchak* also took place at Pesach time (not Rosh Hashanah). And *Targum Yonasan* writes that the day Yitzchak chose for giving his blessings to his son was the 14th of Nissan, *Erev Pesach*.

Apparently, Yitzchak Avinu is intimately connected with Pesach; but he gets nary a mention at the *seder*, or at any other time over Pesach. Who was this man, and what are we to learn from him?

One of the outstanding Torah teachers of the first years of the 20th century was Rav Nachum Zev Ziv of Kelm. Rav Nachum Zev himself was a great admirer of the Chafetz Chaim, and he once described the Chafetz Chaim's special qualities in this way: "I have met Jews who showed me what it is to be a *gaon* (a giant of Torah learning), and Jews who showed me what it means to be a *tzaddik*; but to show what it means to be a *Jew*, that is the uniqueness of the Chafetz Chaim."

I do not claim to understand the depths of Rav Nachum Zev's statement, but to consider it on a very simple level: In Eastern Europe there was a certain Chassidic *Rav*, a great *tzaddik* who was noted for the special intensity of his prayers. Jews would come from miles around to hear (and watch) him recite *Shema*, at which time he would fall to the floor in a swoon, from feelings of awe at the "acceptance of the yoke of the Kingdom of Heaven."

The visitors were surely inspired by what they witnessed. But when they returned to their villages, they did not all start falling to the floor *en masse* in their daily *davening*. "The Rebbe is a *tzaddik*, the Rebbe is a *malach* (angel), but this is not for us." Quite so. But since the Rebbe is so completely different from us, there is a danger that we will not learn from *his davening* to improve *our own davening* at all. A *malach* inspires; but since we are not *malachim*, he is not a role model.

A young man spends years learning in yeshivos, and he acquires a vision of *gadlus*, Torah greatness, as exemplified by his *Rosh Yeshivah*. Unfortunately, this particular young man ends up becoming not a *Rosh Yeshivah*, but a lawyer or a plumber, and he has no mental picture of great Torah lawyers or plumbers at all, so he stumbles.

Biographies of Torah personalities are goldmines of information and insight, but very few of them are about Jews who were not *Rabbanim* and *Roshei Yeshivah*. Even the exceptions (including biographies of Jewish women) deal mostly with leaders and builders, Holocaust rescuers or Beis Yaakov founders, and very little is written about giants of the spirit who did not accomplish much in the *public* realm. This is not a complaint. An individual's private spiritual life is extraordinarily difficult to write about, and if the subject is not a celebrity it will not attract many readers. But where can I find a Jew like *me* to inspire me, to show what it means to be, not a famous teacher or leader, not an innovator or a builder, but a Jew?

Our fathers Avraham, Yitzchak and Yaakov were chosen by Hashem, they were prophets of the highest level and they attained a holiness that people like ourselves cannot begin to comprehend (see, for instance, Rav Aharon Kotler's *shiur* on how to teach *Chumash*, in *Mishnas Rabbi Aharon* vol. III p. 177). But at the same time, "'*maasei Avos siman labanim*, the deeds of the *Avos* are lessons for their descendants,' meaning that they are lessons teaching the descendants how they should conduct themselves" (ibid.).

This explains the puzzling phenomenon that casual readers find great men and women of *Chumash* committing "sins" that make them appear unworthy, Heaven forbid: "I would never have sent away Yishmael like Sarah did, and I would not have tried to kill Yosef like the brothers did; so why did Hashem choose them and not me?" The real story involved debates among spiritual giants on issues we can only begin to fathom (see *Mishnas Rabbi Aharon*, ibid.). But the Torah's purpose is not to teach history; it is to teach lessons in life for every Jew, including children. The Torah deliberately portrays its heroes in a way that we can learn from them, and we have every right to learn, as long as we keep in mind that the lesson we learn is not the full picture.

"The deeds of the *Avos* are lessons for their descendants." Avraham Avinu discovered Hashem on his own, was opposed by all the world, but triumphed to become a teacher to the world. Founders, innovators, creative thinkers and teachers, every spiritual warrior and every *nesi Elokim* ("prince of G-d") draws strength from our father Avraham.

Yaakov Avinu literally created the people of Israel. He fathered and raised the *shevatim*, 12 sons worthy of being designated as the Twelve Tribes. He contended with Eisav, endured Lavan, wrestled with an angel, and laid the groundwork for the expansion of the family into a nation in Egyptian Exile. Builders and strivers, strategic planners and fighters in titanic struggles — and also parents of large families — all draw strength from our father Yaakov.

But what about the Jew who is not a founder or builder or innovator? And what about the Jew who wishes to serve Hashem with all the strength he or she has, but is "neither a *Rav* nor a *Rosh Yeshivah* nor a Chassidic *Rebbe*, but a plain layman"? Such a Jew is not necessarily less learned or devout — the above quotation is from Rav Aharon Kotler's *hesped* (eulogy) for the Chazon Ish! — but who is *that* Jew's role model among the *Avos*? For that Jew, Hashem gave us the man about whom we say, "*You* are our father": Yitzchak Avinu.

When Avraham prepared to take Yitzchak on the journey to Mt. Moriah to offer him as a sacrifice, he had to tell his wife Sarah where they were going, but he did not wish to frighten her. *Midrash Tanchuma* (*Vayeira*) says that Avraham told her: "There is a place, distant from us, where they train (*mechanchim*) the young men. I will take Yitzchak, and train him there."

Our father Avraham would not have told our mother Sarah a blatant lie. Although he did not know how much longer his son Yitzchak had to live, Avraham understood that this trial was also meant to shape Yitzchak's soul. The Divine command to Avraham was to act. The command, or the "training," for Yitzchak was to accept.

There are times when we are tested where we will exert ourselves to overcome laziness, passion or external circumstances that stand in our way. And there are other times when there is little or nothing we can do, and the test is then to accept, and to make the right choices from among the few options that remain. When the two sons of Moshe's brother Aharon died, "Aharon was silent," and silence was a spiritual achievement for which he was rewarded (*Zevachim* 115b). "Just as I received reward for the teaching, so will I receive reward for the refraining" (*Pesachim* 22b).

It is a peculiarly American fantasy that every problem has a solution. Government declares "War on Poverty," studies the "root causes" of crime, and affirms that the Arab-Israeli conflict will end if only both sides "negotiate." We expect pills to work for every physical and emotional hurt, procedures to succeed in staving off the aging process and death itself, and lawsuits to soothe the pain of any expectations unfulfilled. Eastern Europeans sometimes had bad marriages, and accepted them; we have no bad marriages, only broken ones, after a decent interval of family counseling to see if the problem can be "solved."

It is a rare person who, when he does not know what to do, does not do it; and who, when he does not know what to say, does not say it. To strive to become such a person, consider the model of Yitzchak Avinu.

Beginning with an incident from his later years, Yitzchak Avinu was old, blind, and "does not know the day of his death" (*Genesis* 27:1-2). He had the power to pass on a special blessing to one of his sons, and he selected Eisav. Before Eisav arrives for his appointment, Yaakov (at our mother Rivkah's urging) comes to Yitzchak, masquerading as Eisav to be blessed in his stead.

Yitzchak is suspicious — "the voice is the voice of Yaakov, but the hands are the hands of Eisav" — but he gives the blessing anyway. Yaakov walks out, Eisav walks in, Father Yitzchak discovers he has been fooled, but says, "I blessed him, Indeed, he shall remain blessed" (*Genesis* 27:33).

The numerous questions on this section are well known.

(1) Why did Yitzchak prefer Eisav to Yaakov? It is clear from many sources that Eisav was undeserving, and even that his wickedness was common knowledge (*Bava Basra* 123a, cited in part by *Rashi* on *Genesis* 29:17). If Eisav in his father's presence pretended to be righteous, why did Yitzchak disregard the testimony of everyone else, including his wife Rivkah? The suggestion of the *Ohr Hachaim* and others, that Yitzchak knew the truth but felt it would be better to bless Eisav anyway, answers these questions but raises others.

(2) When Yitzchak sensed that "the voice is the voice of Yaakov," why did he give the blessing without further checking? Why not call in a trusted servant, or anyone who could see?

(3) Yaakov had expressed his fear that if Yitzchak discovered the deception, Yitzchak would curse him. But when the deception was revealed, not only did Yitzchak not express any anger, he gave his full assent: "I blessed him. Indeed he shall remain blessed." If you wish to argue that Yitzchak was not assenting, but merely stating that the matter was out of his hands, what value is there to a blessing obtained under false pretenses in the first place?

The simplest answer is this one: Yitzchak knew who Eisav was. Everyone did. (The verse that Yitzchak loved Eisav because of his hunting does not say he loved Eisav *more* than Yaakov, but that he saw good qualities in Eisav which made him deserving of some blessing, which in the end Eisav did receive.) Given a choice, Yitzchak would certainly have bestowed the special blessing on Yaakov, not Eisav. But the choice was not his to make.

Avraham had two sons, but Hashem had told him, "in Yitzchak will be called your seed" (*Genesis* 21:12), and Avraham therefore knew who should receive his blessings. Hashem had said "*in* Yitzchak" to imply "but not *all* of Yitzchak" (*Nedarim* 31a), so Yitzchak knew that his blessing was to go to only one son, but which one? Hashem had not revealed this to him (Rivkah knew the prophecy that "the elder will serve the younger," but was not permitted to reveal it to Yitzchak, as per *Bereshis Rabbah Vayeishev* 84:19), nor did Yitzchak know that Eisav had sold his birthright to Yaakov. Based on the information he had, Yitzchak must assume the special blessing is for Eisav his firstborn.

Give undeserving Eisav the blessing? Did our father expect his descendants to pray in *Shemonah Esrei* to "*Elokei Avraham, Elokei Yitzchak, v'Elokei Eisav*"? But those are Hashem's questions, not ours. Yitzchak had already long before been to "the place where they train the young men," and he knew that his job was to accept, and to do Hashem's Will as best he knew how, without second-guessing.

When Yitzchak heard "the voice of Yaakov," it aroused his suspicions, and he felt obligated to check by embracing his son and feeling "the hands of Eisav." But he felt no obligation to *double*-check, because if this man was Eisav, well and good, and if it was Yaakov, even better! Yitzchak had always understood that there must be a reason why Hashem had taken away his eyesight; now he recognized the possibility that the reason was "for Yaakov to be able to take the *berachos*" (*Rashi, Genesis* 27:1, from *Midrash Tanchuma*). Yitzchak was still uncertain, but he saw that, either way, by going along with the situation he would ultimately fulfill the Will of Hashem.

When Yitzchak discovered that he had given the blessings to Yaakov, "he trembled a great trembling." He had always thought the chosen people would come from the unworthy Eisav, and he had surely spent much time contemplating the meaning of Hashem's plan and constructing an ideology to fit it (perhaps the chosen people were to come from Eisav just as Avraham came from Terech, and King David from King Balak of Moab). Now, the whole structure of Yitzchak Avinu's "theology," so many *shiurim* and *chiddushim* (lessons and novels insights), came tumbling down as in a house of cards. Yitzchak trembled, but he was not sorry. "I blessed him. Indeed he shall remain blessed," and Yitzchak rejoiced to see that Hashem's Will was done.

"And there was a famine in the land, aside from the first famine that had been in the days of Avraham, and Yitzchak went to Avimelech, king of the Philistines, to Gerar" (*Genesis* 26:1). Hashem arranged for Yitzchak to undergo experiences his father Avraham had, to show us Yitzchak's different approach (not better or worse but different, depending upon the individual person's spiritual personality — *shoresh ha-neshamah* — and the needs of the particular situation). Both Avraham and Yitzchak experienced famine, lived in Gerar, concealed their wives' identities, had problems with Avimelech, and were robbed of their wells by Philistines.

(The following idea — and the inspiration for this chapter — is from the Alter of Slabodka's great disciple Rav Avraham Eliyahu Kaplan published among his collected writing in *Sefer B'Ikvus Hayirah*).

"And Yitzchak's servants dug in the valley, and they found there a well of fresh water. But the shepherds of Gerar quarreled with the shepherds of Yitzchak, saying, 'The water is ours'; so he called the name of the well 'Esek' ('Quarrel') for they had quarreled with him. And they dug another well, and they quarreled over that also; and he called its name 'Sitnah' ('Attack' or 'Accusation,' like the word Satan)" (*Genesis* 26:19-21).

It should not surprise us that Yitzchak Avinu gave names to his wells, as did his father Avraham before him (ibid. 26:18). A well was a source of life for the community, and digging a new well was part of their service of Hashem ("Yitzchak Avinu dug five wells, which correspond to the five Books of the Torah," *Bereshis Rabbah* 64:7). But what *is* surprising is that Yitzchak named two of his wells as he gave them up to others. Who would use these names? Certainly not the Philistines!

But imagine: Philistine shepherds quarrel with Yitzchak's shepherds, trying to rob Yitzchak of his well. Yitzchak had become fabulously wealthy (wealthier than King Avimelech, ibid. 64:6), and he could have put up a fight. The whole town turned out to witness the confrontation and see what the son of Avraham (who had been famous in Gerar, *Genesis* 20:8) would do.

Yitzchak decided that the well was not worth a battle, i.e., it was not Hashem's Will to fight. But before the Philistines and all the assembled neighbors, Yitzchak Avinu said: "This well is a tragic quarrel, a quarrel did not have to be, and it deserves the name *Esek*." When it happened a second time, Yitzchak said, before all assembled: "The first time may have been a lamentable misunderstanding, but a second time? Clearly, this is nothing but *Sitnah*, a mean-spirited attack; and so should this well be named, to remember and take note of such deeds."

The Philistines did not call the wells by those names, but neighbors and travelers did. "Yes, that well is *Esek*, where the prophet Yitzchak protested the evils of *machlokes*, quarreling. And that other well is *Sitnah*, where the prophet proclaimed the revulsion that a noble soul should feel over an unwarranted attack by a neighbor." Avraham had traveled from place to place as the world's teacher, "calling out in the Name of

Hashem." Yitzchak's teachings were much more low key, but at the right place and time were no less effective.

"And Avraham rebuked Avimelech, because of the well that Avimelech's servants had stolen" (ibid. 21:25). Avraham rebuked openly. Yitzchak did so more subtly, almost symbolically.

Avraham's wife Sarah was abducted by Avimelech, and Yitzchak's wife Rivkah was in danger of being abducted by Avimelech (*Rashi, Genesis* 26:10; "Avimelech, My father the king," was a royal title; the two Avimelechs were different men but the Torah does not differentiate between them, because their similarities in character make them the same for all intents and purposes; this is also the Torah's approach with the various Pharaohs). Both Avraham and Yitzchak had said that their wives were their sisters, in both cases Avimelech discovered the truth, and in both cases Avimelech asked for an explanation. Note the differences in their respective replies:

Avraham: "Because I said, only there is no fear of G-d in this place, and they will kill me because of my wife" (ibid. 20:11).

Yitzchak: "Because I said, I might die because of her" (ibid. 26:9).

Avraham was the *Rebbe*, the great teacher, and he explains his actions with a *shiur*, a Torah lecture on Fear of Hashem. Yitzchak speaks as a private person, making his point more subtly ("I might die," instead of "they will kill me") but no less effectively.

In the Gemara *Shabbos* 89b cited earlier, Yitzchak Avinu defends us at the last judgment by arguing that at Mt. Sinai we said *Naaseh* before *Nishma*, and for this Hashem called us His children at that time. But why does only Yitzchak defend us, and not Yaakov or Avraham?

From all the above, the answer is self-evident: The spiritual strengths of Avraham and Yaakov were chiefly in *doing*, creating and building. The chief merit of descendants who follow in their footsteps is also in the good deeds they do, and by sinning their merit is gravely weakened.

But as explained above, the special spiritual strength of Yitzchak Avinu is not in *doing*, but in *accepting*. It is therefore Yitzchak who defends us by reminding Hashem that we *accepted* the Torah on trust, without knowing the details (*Naaseh*, we will do, before *Nishma*, we will hear). Our deeds may be wanting, but Israel still accepts Hashem as our Father. The Gemara thus explains the verse in *Isaiah* 63:16 this way: The Jewish people will say, "for *you* (Yitzchak) are our father, for Avraham did not know us, and Yisrael (Yaakov) did not acknowledge us; *You, Hashem*, are our Father ..."; our link to our father on earth (Yitzchak, by our remaining the people who accept) maintains our link to our Father in Heaven.

Yitzchak Avinu was born in the month of Nissan, not because Nissan is Pesach time, but the reverse: Hashem planned Pesach in Nissan in order to fall out on Yitzchak Avinu's birthday. The Pesach *seder* is "the place where we train the young men" (and women too) in what it means to be a Jew; not necessarily a *gaon* and *tzaddik* — three of the four sons do not fit that description — but the essence of being a *Yid*. That essence is:

"Hashem our G-d took us out of Egypt with a mighty hand and outstretched arm, and had He not done so, we would still be slaves." We could never have freed ourselves on our own, and whatever we may achieve in our lives today will not be achieved on our own. We do all we can, including every mitzvah up to the *afikoman*. But the core of Pesach night is the *korban*, the Pesach lamb; a symbol that we are the sheep, Hashem is the shepherd, and we accept His guidance as did our father, the "lamb" brought on Mt. Moriah. And in eating the lamb (which we cannot do today) we recall the deliverance; how Hashem saved our father and sent a ram to be offered in his place, the ram of our father Yitzchak.

COVENANT AND COMMUNITY

A question in political science: If the people of the United States wish to pass a new law or to change an old one, in most cases a majority vote of their elected representatives in both houses of Congress will suffice to effect the change. If, however, the proposed change affects any law in the federal Constitution, then even a unanimous vote is not enough. Changing the Constitution requires a laborious and time-consuming process involving most of the states, a process which may drag on for years, as required by the rules set down in the Constitution itself.

The question is: America's Constitution is over 200 years old. Its creators are all long dead, and none of us alive today had any say in its creation. How, then, can all of us today be bound by such a document, and is it morally *right* to be bound by such a document, to which we did not consent? This is a famous question to which there is no thoroughly satisfactory answer, except to say that the American system of government, flawed as it is, is probably superior to most other systems the pre-Messianic era has to offer.

Now, to consider, *lehavdil*, the constitution of the Jewish nation, our Torah: Hashem gave us the Torah only after asking for our ancestors' consent, which they gave enthusiastically ("*Naaseh v'nishma*, we will do and we will listen") more than 3,300 years ago. But if the Torah was only given with the recipients' consent back then, why is the Torah still binding on every Jew today, consenting or not? There is no question that all Jews are bound by the Torah (*Deuteronomy* 29:14), and whether or not we understand *why* we are obligated does not affect the obligation itself. But as part of our obligation to learn and try to understand the Torah, it is a worthy question to ask, how the original ancestral consent at Mt. Sinai continues to obligate us today. (Special thanks to Reb Avi Shulman of Monsey, New York, for raising this question in one of his newsletters.)

There is no "official" answer to this question in *Tanach* or Gemara, but there is the famous Gemara (*Shabbos* 146a) that at the giving of the Torah the souls of all Israel were present at Mt. Sinai, including the souls of Jews yet unborn. This would answer our question by saying that obligation does indeed require personal consent, but all of us gave consent when our souls joined the chorus of commitment at the very beginning.

Two minor objections to using this Gemara as "the" answer: (1) It is surprising that such a fundamental principle (and what is more fundamental than our obligation to keep the Torah?) is not more clearly explained. The Gemara itself is referring to future converts to Judaism, not future Jewish descendants. *Sifsei Chachamim* (*Deuteronomy* 29:14) writes that the idea of future souls present at Mt. Sinai applies also to Jewish descendants, but he also suggests that the obligation on future generations stems from a completely different source, i.e. that "the son is the foot of the father," an explanation which requires an explanation itself. (2) One might argue that it is unfair for unborn souls to accept obligations, because souls do not suffer temptations of the flesh, and had we been present with both body and soul together we might not have accepted at all!

A different approach was suggested by the famous Torah philosopher Dr. Isaac Breuer. His answer was that the Torah was not given to individual Jews, but to the Jewish nation as a whole; and anyone who is part of the nation becomes subject to its laws.

By way of analogy, foreign visitors to the United States cannot exempt themselves from the obligations of American law. If they are *here*, they are subject to the laws. In the same way, being a Jew (by birth or conversion) means to be part of the Nation of Hashem, a nation whose essence is defined not by territorial boundaries or language and culture, but by the national covenant with Hashem. If you are Jewish, if you are part of this nation of the covenant, you are then bound by Torah law. Whether or not you possess religious "faith," it is sufficient that a "citizen" must obey national law.

Dr. Breuer's explanation leads naturally to the question: May one renounce one's citizenship, and resign from the Jewish Nation? The Torah says it is not possible. When the Torah warns us that the soul of the wicked is cut off (*kares*), it sometimes says "the soul will be cut off from before Me." The Midrash explains: You might think that a Jewish soul cut off from Israel could find a resting place elsewhere. The Torah therefore says, "cut off from before Me," cut off from Hashem, from everywhere that is; because for a Jew, outside the Jewish people there is no place else.

These are deep waters. But even on the simplest level of understanding, Shavuos is a time to remind us that we accepted the Torah as part of a people, all of us in it together. At Sinai, Hashem gave His Torah to a *tzibbur*, a community, and it is only as a community that the Torah can be fully lived.

We often tend to think of the Jewish community in terms of institutions which provide us with services (*shuls*, yeshivos, *chesed* organizations), or who need our help to enable them to provide service for others. But above and beyond the needs of worthy Jewish institutions, the *neshamah*, the Jewish soul, is incomplete without the community, for many reasons.

One reason why we need one another is that no single person can fulfill all 613 mitzvos. A Kohen cannot perform the mitzvah of burying the dead, and a non-Kohen cannot fulfill the Kohen's mitzvah of avoiding contact with the dead. Not everyone has a firstborn son to redeem, and not everyone will commit a robbery in order to have the mitzvah of returning a stolen object. By being part of the Jewish Nation, the mitzvos of all Jews are a collective accomplishment, and we receive some credit for the good deeds of all Israel (for the bad deeds, we also share in the blame, but on balance we end up far ahead).

A second reason why we need our community is that people on their own run the risk of becoming more than a little *meshuga*. Just as solitary confinement sometimes drives prisoners insane, so too religious solitude, being alone without other sincere Jews with whom to compare notes, can cause people to go astray without realizing it. "Make for yourself a teacher, and acquire for yourself a friend" (*Avos* 1:6).

One example is the young man or woman from a Torah-observant home who pursues a university education in another state, and who abandons Jewish observance along the way. When this occurs the cause is usually not because the student faced difficult philosophical challenges, but because the student lacked a network of emotional and spiritual support, observant friends and teachers at hand to keep them afloat.

The other extreme is the person who sincerely seeks spirituality, but who is not part of a group of friends and teachers. Without a community we can end up engaging in the most self-destructive behavior without realizing it, which is why the Chazon Ish wrote in a letter to a yeshivah student to "beware of doing anything different from all your friends, and to be especially careful about this." Of course, if our peer group does not share Torah ideals then we must act differently from them, but it is then vital to seek out a different peer group of which to become a part.

Yet another reason why belonging to a community is important is that people in close-knit communities end up doing a great deal of good out of feelings of embarrassment in front of their neighbors. The ethical classic *Chovos Halevavos* states that a sense of shame is the major factor encouraging us to give *tzedakah* and honor our parents and help our neighbors and much, much more. As Rav Yitzchak Hutner put it: "Once a town has two *shuls*, a Jew then has the option of attending neither" (heard from Rav Avigdor Miller). Ideally, we should always do the right thing for the right reasons. But — especially when we truly desire to do the right thing, but we are weak — it is better to do good out of embarrassment than not to do good at all.

In *Parshas Yisro*, immediately before the giving of the Torah, the *Chumash* (*Exodus* 18:21) tells how Moshe Rabbeinu set up an extensive system of officers and leaders for Israel; "*sarei alafim sarei meios sarei chamishim v'sarei asaros*, leaders for every 1000 people, for every 100, every 50 and every 10." It was a complete structure, each Jew belonging to "a little platoon" which was part of a larger group, and every 10 Jews had their own leader, someone to encourage you, and to remind you to uphold your own ideals.

Shavuos, when we reaffirm our personal commitment to the *Bris*, the Covenant of Sinai, is a time to reaffirm our commitment to the Community of Sinai as well. Whether attending more *shiurim* or giving more *tzedakah*, *davening* with a *minyan* or showing concern for a neighbor, we should recognize that in building a community, we are truly building ourselves. Saying *Yizkor* is also a reminder that our community goes back in time, and we are still linked to those who are gone. Their memories are part of us, and we pledge *tzedakah* at *Yizkor* to show that they continue to inspire us in the way we act today.

It is said that after the great Rav Yisrael Salanter passed away, a certain Jew came into possession of Rav Yisrael's hat. The hat was old, creased and faded, but the new owner always made a point to wear it on Shabbos. He said: "With Rav Yisrael Salanter's hat on my head, I find that I simply cannot speak *lashon hara*."

We all wear the hats of our parents and grandparents, and to some extent all of us are wrapped in the clothing of the community in which we live. By focusing on the right memories, and bringing ourselves closer to the right friends and neighbors, we can clothe ourselves in true garments of Yom Tov, garments in which to receive the Torah, and rejoice with it through the year.

CELESTIAL DEBATE

O n Yom Tov, one opinion in the Gemara (*Pesachim* 68b) is that we are to spend half the day learning Torah, and the other half eating and drinking; "*chatzi l'Hashem v'chatzi lachem*, half the day for Hashem and the other half for yourselves." A second opinion disagrees, arguing that it is proper to spend the entire day in Torah-study alone, *kulo l'Hashem*, all for Hashem.

The Gemara concludes, "*Hakol modim b'atzeres b'inan nami lachem*" — all agree that on Shavuos, at least part of the day must be spent eating and drinking. Why? "*Yom shenitnah Torah l'Yisrael*, Shavuos is the day the Torah was given to the people of Israel." This conclusion is difficult to understand; surely Shavuos, the day the Torah was given, should be a day of learning above all other days! Why then does the Gemara say that Shavuos must include food and drink more than other Yamim Tovim, precisely *because* it was the day the Torah was given?

When Moshe Rabbeinu ascended Mt. Sinai to receive the Torah, he attained a level of prophecy which the Gemara calls "entering Heaven." Moshe entered Heaven on behalf of the Jewish people and stood before the Creator's throne, surrounded by the ministering angels; and the angels made a protest. "*Mah liyelud ishah beineinu,* How dare a frail human being come among us?" They wanted to kill Moshe, to "burn him with the breath of their mouths."

At that point, the Midrash tells us, Hashem transformed Moshe's face, to make him look like our father Avraham. Hashem then said to the angels: "You wish to kill this man? You should feel ashamed to appear before him! When you visited him, you ate meat and milk together!" This refers to the three angels who visited Avraham (*Genesis* 18:8), and to whom Avraham served cream and milk and the meat of a calf. When the angels heard this they relented, and agreed that Moshe Rabbeinu should be given the Torah.

What does this Midrash mean? Are angels so easily fooled that instant plastic surgery makes them believe that Moshe is not Moshe but Avraham? And as to their apparently non-kosher lunch, if angels are not supposed to eat milk and meat together, why did they do so? Celestial beings do not lust after cheeseburgers. And if it was wrong to eat, why did our father Avraham serve it to them? The Gemara tells us that Avraham kept the entire Torah even before it was given. Why then would he cause other people to sin?

In the observance of almost every mitzvah, some of the mitzvah's *halachos* (laws) come from the Torah itself, while other details of halachah were added by the Rabbis. Both types of *halachos* are equally binding, but there is a distinct qualitative difference between them. Whatever the Torah itself forbids is something which is intrinsically harmful, injurious to the soul. A prohibition added later by the Rabbis is not necessarily something which is dangerous in itself, but is usually a precaution to keep us from violating the Biblical commandment. For instance, the Torah forbids eating milk and meat that were cooked together; for reasons unknown to us, consuming milk and meat in the same mouthful does spiritual damage. But the Rabbis proceeded to add a prohibition against eating milk even *after* meat, recognizing that this was needed to protect the original mitzvah and keep it intact through the generations.

Every Rabbinic safeguard is a reflection of human weakness, that we require a protective fence to guard us from temptation. But at the same time, these safeguards demonstrate a yearning to *overcome* that weakness, that the Jewish people will not permit themselves to be defeated. For this reason the Rabbis say that *"chavivin divrei sofrim yoser miyeina shel Torah*, laws of the Sages are more beloved to Hashem than even the mitzvos of the Torah"; because the laws of the Sages express our concern that the Torah is dear enough to us to fight to protect it.

Our father Avraham was a *navi*, a prophet. He understood and observed all the laws of the Torah, Biblical *and* Rabbinic. When he was visited by angels disguised as Arabs, Avraham would not serve them Biblically forbidden food, but he did not rerain from serving foods which are Rabbinically prohibited, which are not intrinsically harmful. Although Avraham kept those laws himself, why should he make things difficult for these Arabs by insisting that *they* keep the safeguards, safeguards for Torah mitzvos they do not observe anyway? So he served them milk and meat, not together, but at the same meal.

The angels said to themselves, looking from their own point of view: "We would not transgress a mitzvah of the Torah. But Rabbinic laws are enacted to cope with human weakness, to keep flesh and blood far from temptation. We angels need not worry about such weakness, and we can disregard *halachos* of the Rabbis." So they ate meat and milk at the same meal, though not together in the same mouthful.

Centuries later, when Moshe Rabbeinu came to receive the Torah, the angels argued, How does a frail human being dare to enter Heaven? The Creator responded: Moshe is indeed a frail human being, just as Avraham before him was a frail human being. But because of that very frailty, Avraham and

Moshe and the Sages and the Jewish nation set up safeguards, Rabbinic laws to protect the Torah, efforts to overcome their weaknesses and draw closer to Hashem despite the struggle. You angels did not keep those additional laws because you do not need them, you are computer programed to be perfect. But the sanctity of a human being who suffers temptation, who falls in the dirt and yet rises again and again — angels have nothing to approach *that* greatness. In the presence of Avraham's loyal children, even angels feel ashamed of how insignificant they are by comparison.

And this is why the Torah did not remain in Heaven, but was given to human beings, even to insignificant human beings like ourselves. This is also a reason for the custom of eating dairy foods on Shavuos, in order to demonstrate that we keep all the Rabbinic laws separating milk and meat, which is how we merited to receive the Torah in the first place. And it also explains the Gemara's statement that on Shavuos, all agree that at least some time must be devoted to food and drink; because on Shavuos it is not enough to act like an angel. Shavuos is when we demonstrate the greatness of being *human*, that we can eat and drink and celebrate in accordance with all the *halachos* of the Torah; because Torah is not for angels, it is for all of us, if we only make the effort to begin.

The Gemara (*Shabbos* 88b-89a) tells another story of Moshe Rabbeinu and the angels, that Moshe answered their objections by asking: "Are *you* tempted by the desire to rob and murder, that you need a mitzvah of Thou shalt not steal, Thou shalt not kill?" That story is in essence almost identical to the story in the above Midrash, with a slightly different emphasis. Many people, including some of the most sensitive souls, find themselves troubled by a feeling that the Torah is not really for them, or at least certain mitzvos are not for them, because "they're just not that religious," "not frum enough." But the Gemara here is telling us that the Torah is not intended for naturally religious people, not for saintly, angelic people who are never tempted to kill or steal. Torah was designed from the beginning for irreligious folks, Jews who are not so *frum*, including Jews like us;

to challenge us, to push us, and to elevate us to the unique sort of greatness only Jews like us can achieve.

Shavuos is the day Hashem gave us His Torah, more than 3,300 years ago. Shavuos is also the day for us to *receive* the Torah, to accept it this year, here and now. If we can only comprehend that the Torah is here to confront each of us with personal challenges that are not always comfortable, but are always uniquely *ours*, we can then begin to wrestle with the mitzvos and with ourselves.

Sometimes we will win, other times not. But, as we see even in non-Jewish society, the world's most popular spectator sport, for which many millions of fans pay huge sums of money for tickets, is prizefighting, heavyweight boxing matches. Savage as such entertainment is, the worldwide excitement over it is not merely a desire for bloodshed, or a desire to throw a vicarious punch at the tax collector. The thrill stems from an inner feeling, an emotional realization that to be in the arena, to struggle and to fall but to refuse to be counted out until the final bell — that is the core of a meaningful life.

Sadly, the world around us has no knowledge of the true prizes worth fighting for. But we, who have been blessed with that knowledge, for us Shavuos is a day to celebrate, feasting with joy for our Torah; and knowing that in all our struggles, even angels cheer us on, because in Heaven they recognize that human struggle is an honor, and a sanctity uniquely our own.

THE LIMITS OF BEING A REALIST

O ver 33 centuries ago, our ancestors came to the foot of Mt. Sinai, and the Creator of the Universe asked if they would accept the commandments of His Torah. They replied: *"Kol asher diber Hashem, naaseh v'nishma,* Everything G-d has spoken, we will do, and we will listen." This means that even before they heard precisely what all the mitzvah obligations were, they accepted them, and agreed to fulfill them; from that acceptance they would then go on to study the details.

The Gemara (*Shabbos* 88a) tells us that when the Jewish people made that reply, Hashem looked down in happiness and said: "Who revealed this secret to My children, the secret the ministering angels use?" — to say first "we will do," and only afterwards "we will listen."

What is the meaning of this secret, and what it has to do with angels, the Gemara does not tell us. But the Gemara does tell us that a nonbeliever once criticized us: *"Ibai l'chu l'mishma iy matzisu kablisu,"* you Jews should have first said, "We will listen." You should first have heard what the Torah is and whether you will be able to keep it, and only afterwards say "we will do," not the other way around.

The great Rava answered him: When the Book of *Proverbs* (11:3) states that "the faith of the righteous will guide them," that verse applies to us at Mt. Sinai. Another phrase in that verse, "the cunning of the disloyal will destroy them," applies to people like you.

The nonbeliever's argument appears to have been: We Jews should not have accepted the Torah before we knew that we would be able to keep it. Rava's response was that the righteous are guided by their faith, meaning that we trusted Hashem; He would not give us His Torah unless it is something good for us; it is surely in our own best interest to accept the Torah.

However, if this is the true meaning of the Gemara, then the idea it conveys appears to be so self-evident that it hardly seems worthy of being recorded. Since Hashem made us an offer of His Torah, certainly it is something we can keep! It is a given that Hashem loves us, and He states openly that He gave up His Torah to make us His special people, a "kingdom of priests (or: princes) and a holy nation" (*Exodus* 19:6).

No serious person would believe that Hashem asked us to accept mitzvos in order to do us harm. But if the nonbeliever was asking a stupid question, or merely throwing insults, the Gemara would not have bothered to record them for posterity. Surely the question, and Rava's answer, included a depth beyond the surface reading. Perhaps the meaning is:

The nonbeliever argued: Your acceptance of the Torah would have been much greater, much more meaningful, if you had first heard what the Torah *is*. First know what you are getting, learn it, comprehend the breadth and depth of its responsibilities, and *then* accept it; that would be a powerful commitment to Hashem. But to sign a contract without bothering to first read it? "*Naaseh v'nishma*, we'll do whatever it is, and later we'll hear the details" shows an impetuous lack of thought, a lack of seriousness in your pledge.

That argument has merit. It is worthy of being recorded, and of receiving a response. How did Rava respond? "The faith of the righteous will guide them. The cunning of the disloyal will destroy them," which means: Sometimes, you can be too cunning, too smart for your own good.

As the English essayist Thomas Carlyle once expressed it, "Every great thing is at first impossible." Imagine if we could explain to our teenagers all the difficulties of marriage, all the responsibilities and all the hardships of raising a family and creating a home — would any young person ever choose to get married? Years later, the happily married man and woman look back and say it was all well worth it; but to know of all the problems in advance and willingly accept them? Unlikely.

What is true of marriage is true of adulthood in general, and of most areas of achievement, from making a living to serving the Jewish community. Looking back, the rewards were worth all the difficulties; but had you known of them in advance, you would never have become involved.

The Torah is not merely a "religion," a set of comfortable beliefs and ceremonies to provide a sense of order and add dignity to special occasions. Torah is the superconductor, the Divine energy to connect us with holiness and to transform a stiff-necked people into a kingdom of priests and princes. To become the am segulah and ohr lagoyim, the treasured people and a light to all the nations of the world, remains a daunting challenge even after all these centuries have passed. But at the start, had they perceived the totality of the Torah's mission before they accepted it, they would have said: It cannot be done.

And therefore Rava explained: The only way, Hakadosh Baruch Hu's way, was to let "the faith of the righteous guide us." To say, Hashem, you know best. Naaseh v'nishma. First, before we even hear it, we commit ourselves. We will do. Not "we will try." Not "we will do our best." But we will do, period, we will keep the Torah, we will succeed, and on this there is no question at all.

And the Gemara reveals to us that *this* approach is the se-cret of the angels. When a prophet announces his prophetic message, he says "*Ko amar Hashem*, thus says the Lord"; but an angel who relates Hashem's word typically says, "*Ani*, I say." Both are only quoting the Master, but the angel says "*ani*, I," because the entire essence of the angel is only the Will of Hashem. The angel has no personal will, and it goes without saying that the angel's "I" is a quotation, because all that the angel is and says is only from Hashem. That com-plete negation of self, that he knows nothing but the Divine Will, and the Divine Word is all that is, that is the secret, the source of the angel's enormous power. There are no obsta-cles, because in the path of Hashem roadblocks cannot even be conceived.

We are not angels. But Rav Yosef Yoizel Horvitz of Novardok, whose disciples founded more than 80 yeshivos in Russia and Poland, used to say: "I never ask whether a particular project *can* be done, only whether it *should* be done. If it *should* be done, I go ahead, and I am confident that the means to suc-ceed will be found."

I have not been able to verify the authenticity of the fol-lowing story in all its details, but several similar incidents occurred in the lives of other 20th-century builders of Torah, and the core of the story is certainly worth sharing:

Rav Yosef Kahaneman, the last Rav of the Lithuanian town of Ponovezh, arrived in *Eretz Yisrael* during the Second World War. His family had been murdered, his community turned to ashes, and the German panzer Afrika Korps was at the gates of Egypt. But the Ponovezher Rav saw an empty hilltop in the little village of Bnei Brak, and he said: "On that hilltop, I will build a yeshivah as a memorial to Ponovezh; a Torah center with hundreds and hundreds of students, even larger than the great yeshivos of prewar Eastern Europe."

Some of his friends said: "*Nebach*, with all the tragedies the old rabbi has suffered, his mind has finally broken from the strain." The story goes that they took him to see a psychia-trist, who reportedly said: "Well, at least he's harmless."

That is what happens when you are the only sane person in the asylum. Because Rav Kahaneman understood: When you go to do the Will of Hashem, you do not begin with a feasibility study, and you do not sit down to think of all the reasons why you cannot succeed. Instead, you say *Naaseh V'nishma*, we will *do*, and afterwards we will try to understand. And Rav Kahaneman went on to create *Eretz Yisrael's* largest yeshivah, with branches and affiliate schools of a magnitude unmatched since the days of the Gemara. It seemed utterly impossible; but as Hashem said at Mt. Sinai, there's a secret to it, known only to a few.

Shavuos, *zman matan Toraseinu*, the time of the giving of *our* Torah, is a time to renew our personal commitment to making the Torah truly ours. When inspiration to make any personal spiritual improvement comes our way, we so often tell ourselves that "I'm no *tzaddik*," "I'm too old to make changes," "It's just not me," or "Be realistic."

There are a thousand logical reasons to do nothing, but all those reasons are wrong; because in every sort of personal success there exists an energy to be tapped which goes beyond day-to-day logic. Science tells us that we use only a small fraction of our mental powers. To dig for the power hidden within, and to reach for Divine assistance to develop it, we must begin by reaffirming *Naaseh v'nishma*, we are going to do *something*. One new mitzvah, one additional page of Torah learning, one small step to strengthen a marriage or a career or even an exercise program — progress of every type begins by forgetting all the reasons why the thing cannot be done, and instead making a commitment to do. "Success comes in cans, not can'ts."

And by ignoring limitations and diving in to *naaseh*, to do, we will soon discover that *nishma*, we *will* be able to hear; to comprehend what Hashem wanted for us, how He helps us succeed, and who is the person of achievement each of us is meant to become.

WHY AN OMER?

The Torah does not assign a specific calendar date for the Yom Tov of Shavuos. Instead, it commands us to count 49 days from the bringing of the *Omer*, and the 50th day is Shavuos. The 50th day may or may not be the sixth day of Sivan, depending on whether that year's month of Nissan had 29 or 30 days, which varied when proclaiming the New Moon depended on the testimony of witnesses. Clearly, there is a connection between Shavuos and the counting of the *Omer*.

The most well-known explanation of this connection (found in *Sefer Hachinuch*, and elsewhere) is that when our ancestors left Egypt, Moshe Rabbeinu informed them that in seven weeks they would come to Mt. Sinai, where Hashem would speak to them and give them His Torah. In anticipation of the event, our ancestors began to count the days and weeks — "49 days, seven weeks, 48 days, six weeks and six days to go" — to the great day of Divine Revelation, the day we commemorate on Shavuos.

This explains why Shavuos follows a *counting*. However, it

does not explain why Shavuos follows the counting of the *Omer*. What is the connection between the *Omer* itself, and Shavuos?

The *Omer* was an offering of barley brought in the *Beis Hamikdash*, the Holy Temple, on the second day of Pesach. Grain in *Eretz Yisrael* grows during the winter rainy season, and is harvested shortly before Pesach. The *Omer* offering was brought on Pesach (first day of *Chol Hamoed*, in *Eretz Yisrael*) as an expression of gratitude to Hashem for the new crop.

The Hebrew word *Omer* is a measurement of volume, about two quarts, and it is the volume that the Torah commands to be brought for the barley offering. There is something odd about this which is seldom considered: Why does the Torah, and why do the Jewish people, call this offering by the name *Omer*? The *size* of the offering is only one aspect of it, and it hardly appears to be the most important aspect. I might have named it "The Barley Offering," or "The New Crop Offering," *Korban Hase'orim* or *Korban Hechadash*. Why call it *Omer*, the offering of this particular size?

So now we have two questions: What connection is there between Shavuos and the *Omer* itself, and why is the *Omer* offering named for its size?

When our ancestors left Egypt, and they needed food in the Wilderness, Hashem gave them the miracle food *mon* (manna). The Torah tells us that an additional miracle was that each person ended up with the same amount of *mon* as everyone else, no more and no less. What was that amount? "*Omer lagulgoles*" (*Exodus* 16:16), the volume of an *Omer* for each person.

So we could suggest (and I am indebted to Rabbi Yitzchak Etshalom of Los Angeles for the idea), that when the Torah commands that the offering is to be an *Omer*, the Torah is teaching us that the *Omer* offering should serve to remind us how Hashem took care of our ancestors in the Wilderness. Each year, when we feel the joy of thanksgiving for the new harvest, it is also an opportunity to remember the past, and give thanks for the miracle of the *mon*, the *Omer* sent daily from Heaven for every Jew, for 40 years.

So now we know why the barley offering is called by the name *Omer*, to bring to mind the *Omer*, that particular measurement, of *mon*. To return to our first question: In what way is Shavuos connected to counting days of the *Omer*?

Even in our time, the 49 days between Pesach and Shavuos are meant to be days of spiritual preparation. After the first Pesach, our ancestors prepared to receive the Torah directly from Hashem. And we, in each generation, are also to use these days to prepare for Shavuos, to personally accept the Torah upon ourselves, each year anew. (For example, Rav Aharon Kotler taught that the first 48 days of counting are days to work at developing the 48 *kinyanim*, the 48 paths to acquiring Torah listed in *Pirkei Avos* (*Ethics of Our Fathers*), with the 49th day — *Erev Shavuos* — devoted to reviewing and fashioning the 48 ways into one unified whole.)

But anyone who tries to sincerely accept the Torah finds himself facing formidable obstacles: habit, laziness, lust, arrogance, and, perhaps, above all, a deep-seated fear of change. If I fully commit myself to what the Torah wants of me, what radical changes might I have to eventually make in my life–style? What familiar behavior patterns and comfortable prejudices will I have to abandon? What if certain mitzvos, or serious Torah learning, are just too difficult? Thoughtful people will have many concerns, questioning whether they can truly commit themselves to the entire Torah.

And to answer those questions, and to cope with the fears, the Torah commands us to prepare for Shavuos by counting the days *of the Omer*. Count 49 days to recall the 49 days the Jewish people journeyed to Mt. Sinai for the first Shavuos. They traveled in the Wilderness, and they did not have food; but Hashem gave them an *Omer*, an exact measurement of *mon* to meet their needs. And that is to teach us:

If your destination is Mt. Sinai, if you want to come to the Torah and the promised land, then Hashem will always give you what you require to get where you need to go.

Once when the Vilna Gaon was away from home for an extended period, he wrote a letter to his wife. This letter is known today as *Igeres HaGra*. One of the points in the letter was his urging that his wife take care to maintain all the stringencies to which they had been accustomed. Even if keeping their high standards involved great expense, she should not compromise, because, he wrote, Hashem gives His creatures what they need; and he quoted a *pasuk*, how Hashem provided for us in the Wilderness of Sinai, "*Hayad Hashem tiktzor*, is Hashem's Hand too short to reach?" (*Numbers* 11:23).

I might have argued that what Hashem did 3,000 years ago for Moshe Rabbeinu is no guarantee that He will do the same for us today. I might also have argued that, although Hashem gives His creatures what they need, this refers to *needs*, necessities of life, but it does not follow that He will grant us all we need to remain on the highest levels of spirituality. But the Vilna Gaon says NO, Hashem's help is in every generation. And the Gaon is saying that if it is truly your goal to reach a higher spiritual level, that is *your* necessity; and Hashem will give you what you need to attain it.

One afternoon when I was printing out one of these chapters on my word processor, the computer printer suddenly ran out of ink. *Baruch Hashem*, I had a spare ink cartridge, so I shut the printer off, and lifted the printer cover to replace the cartridge. To my chagrin, I found the old cartridge situated deep inside the printer in a way that was impossible to remove. I saw no way to reach the cartridge without smashing the printer in two, but I knew there must be some more cost-effective alternative.

A friend finally showed me the simple solution to my extraordinarily vexing problem. The ink cartridge truly *is* impossible to replace — as long as the printer is shut off. But turn the printer *on*, let the electric power begin to flow, and the ink cartridge automatically slides down a track out of its corner, in full view to be easily replaced.

To arrive at our personal Mt. Sinai, we need a great many things; things of the spirit and the emotions, and often physical and financial things as well. But whatever the needs, we prepare by counting 49 days of the *Omer*, 49 days to recall how Hashem gave Israel what *they* needed to reach Sinai; and to impress upon ourselves that, however insurmountable an obstacle may appear, since Hashem created us with Torah in mind, He must have provided the means to get there in the end.

We may not see the solution right away, and the goal may appear to be inextricably beyond our reach. But if we make the attempt, if we turn on the machine to attach ourselves to the power of *limud and kiyum haTorah*, Torah learning and Torah living, we can be assured that Sinai is attainable, with a powerful soul processor whose printer never, never, runs out of ink.

THE MOURNER'S COUNT

Yamim Tovim are celebrated for a day (Yom Kippur), or two (e.g. Shavuos in the Diaspora) or even a week or more (Pesach and Succos). A Yom Tov's duration is not the main yardstick for measuring its importance; but if we find a single holiday, or a single period of observance, that is four times as long as any other Yom Tov, that should certainly make us sit up and take notice.

We do have such a period of observance, the period of semi-mourning commonly known as "*Sefirah.*"

During the *Sefirah* period we refrain from weddings, music and haircuts for at least 33 days according to some *minhagim* (customs), up to 49 days according to others. That is four to six times as long as any Yom Tov. Even the *aveilus* (mourning) for the *Beis Hamikdash* (Holy Temple) before Tishah B'Av lasts only three weeks. What is so special about *Sefirah* that it should be the longest observance of them all?

S*efarim* tell us that the reason for the mourning is that in the second century C.E., about 50 years after the destruction of the *Beis Hamikdash*, Rabbi Akiva's 24,000 disciples died in a plague. The death of 24,000 transmitters of the chain of Torah tradition was a terrible tragedy. But when the Romans destroyed Jerusalem and the Second *Beis Hamikdash*, they murdered far more than 24,000, and when Babylon conquered Jerusalem the first time, they did the same. Why are three weeks before Tishah B'Av sufficient mourning for those many hundreds of thousands of victims, while seven weeks are set aside for the 24,000?

The *Aruch Hashulchan* writes: "These days between Pesach and Shavuos have been accepted by all Israel for many centuries as days of tragedy and mourning, for in this brief time period there died the 12,000 pairs of Sages who were Rabbi Akiva's disciples... We also see that the main anti-Semitic persecutions in centuries past in France and Germany were in these days... and there are also other reasons... Therefore, it has been the custom of all Israel, since the days of the *Geonim*, not to marry between Pesach and Shavuos..." (*Orach Chaim* 493).

Sefirah mourning has been "the custom of all Israel, since the days of the *Geonim*" (7th to 10th centuries C.E.). But one reason for this mourning is to lament the persecutions in France and Germany, which began with the First Crusade in 1096! How could one of the reasons for instituting a mourning period be in order to commemorate a tragedy that had not yet occurred?

A possible explanation:
When Jerusalem and the *Beis Hamikdash* were destroyed the first time, the prophets established days to fast and to lament. After the second destruction, the mourning period was strengthened, and possibly extended. As time passed, the Sages saw new troubles to follow those, all the bitterness of Exile and Dispersion until the Final Redemption to come. The deaths of the 24,000 disciples were only a beginning. The Sages foresaw that there would be many more.

Create a new fast day for each new tragedy? There are not enough days in the calendar. And therefore the Jewish people, guided by the Torah Sages, voluntarily accepted upon themselves a time of semi-mourning as a remembrance and a response to all the suffering that occurred since the destruction of Jerusalem and the Second *Beis Hamikdash*. The *Sefirah* period was established as a time to mourn for all the sorrows of the Exile, both sorrows of the past and sorrows yet to come.

They understood that there would be more tragedy, and many different kinds of tragedy, and they therefore established not one day of mourning, and not even an entire week of "*Shivah*"; but they set aside seven weeks, seven days times seven, an entire cycle of time.

And this period was to be not merely a time for prayer or public ceremonies, to say a few words and then go about our business. Instead, they decreed a remembrance of changes in behavior, a visible disruption of patterns of celebration; no weddings, no music, not even the cutting of hair. Because of this, all our planning of joyous occasions, all year round, serve to remind us: "Don't forget *Sefirah*!"

"Mazel tov! You're planning a spring wedding? Before or after *Sefirah*?" "The yeshivah's annual dinner in May? Let's plan the entertainment, because, of course, we can't have music in *Sefirah*." "Pesach is coming, get your haircut, before *Sefirah*."

These restrictions are not terribly dramatic, not nearly as theatrical as a siren or a moment of silence. But in our daily lives they are far more pervasive, more embracing, and more real. Shavuos completes a period of mourning for the 24,000 disciples who died in the second century, and for victims of Persian massacres in the sixth century, the murders of the Crusades in the 11th century, expulsion from Spain in the 15th, burnings at the stake in Poland in the 18th, Czarist pogroms in the 19th, Arab terror and even — dare we say? — the Holocaust in the 20th.

Many people to whom the memory of the Holocaust is so grievously dear do not wish to include it together with other tragedies. They feel that the honor of the Holocaust martyrs demands that their suffering and martyrdom be seen as unique. But, with the greatest sympathy for those whose sufferings the rest of us cannot begin to comprehend, if the Holocaust is left to stand alone with no link to our history, it also loses much of its power to point the way to any sort of meaningful Jewish future. As important as it is to teach our children what happened during the Holocaust, we must also teach them to connect it to the Jewish past, and to know that there will indeed *be* a Jewish future.

The *Sefirah* period comes to an end with Shavuos, the Yom Tov of receiving the Torah and becoming the chosen people ("Who chose us from all the nations and gave us His Torah" — *Birchos HaTorah*). Although Shavuos today always falls on the 6th day of the month of Sivan, the Torah does not date Shavuos that way. Instead, the Torah says that Shavuos is the day after the completion of *Sefirah*. When the 49 days of *Sefirah* end, Shavuos begins.

The "*Sefirah*" in the Torah refers to counting, not mourning. But since Hashem knows the future and includes it in the Divine Plan (as we see, for example, how Rav Saadiah Gaon writes that the mitzvah of *shofar* is to remind us of several milestones in our history, including events that occurred centuries after the Torah was given), we have a right to suggest that there is a direct connection between Shavuos and *Sefirah* mourning as well.

It is only after 49 days of *Sefirah* that Shavuos begins. Perhaps this is to hint to us that all our suffering was not in vain. We do not know the details of Hashem's Plan, and I do not offer explanations why any particular tragedy occurs. But the Torah is hinting: The 49 days, all the days of sorrow, *lead on to something*. The suffering has shaped this people, like the furnace shapes the steel, and this too is part of the covenant which has made us a chosen people.

Orison Swett Marden, an American (non-Jewish) author, wrote in 1894: "It is opposition that develops in us the very power by which we overcome. Without opposition we could never have braced and fortified ourselves, as the oak is braced and anchored for its thousand battles with the tempest. Our trials and sorrows and griefs develop us, in a similar way.

"The man who has triumphed over difficulties bears the signs of victory in his face. An air of triumph is seen in every movement.

"Almost from the dawn of history, oppression has been the lot of the Hebrews; yet they have given the world its noblest songs, its wisest proverbs, its sweetest music. With them, persecution seems to bring prosperity. They thrive, where others would starve."

We do not seek out oppression. But, just as the word *Sefirah* literally means counting, we do know that even oppression counts for something. Shavuos is the day that makes it all worthwhile, the day we received the noblest songs and wisest proverbs and sweetest music, and the promise of ultimate victory, from Hashem.

CURIOUS CUSTOMS

"I n the days of *Sefirah* (counting of the *Omer*, from Pesach to Shavuos), the disciples of Rabbi Akiva died over a period of 33 days; therefore, the custom is to follow certain mourning practices, that we do not marry or cut hair.

"There are different customs as to the reckoning of these 33 days" (*Kitzur Shulchan Aruch,* 120:6). Some observe the mourning period during the 33 days from Pesach to Lag B'Omer, and then mourning comes to an end, while others observe mourning during the last 33 days of the *Omer* period, permitting weddings and haircutting for a full week after Pesach. A third custom is to include every day between Pesach and Shavuos with the exception of festive days, i.e. all of Pesach, all days of Rosh Chodesh and every Shabbos, which leaves 33 days. There are also slight variations within each of the three approaches, e.g., some who observe the last 33 days end the mourning on the third day before Shavuos and therefore begin the mourning period two days earlier (see *Mishnah Berurah* 493).

What is going on here? It is true that Jews are used to different Jewish communities following different customs, but where do we find differences like these, in which different communities (and families) practice their observances on different *weeks?* Some have suggested that the different practices reflect different opinions as to when Rabbi Akiva's disciples died, a highly unusual halachic-historical controversy which would not explain some of the variant customs (see *Igros Moshe Orach Chaim* 159).

A simpler explanation would be to say that the disciples died over a 33–day period between Pesach and Shavuos — not necessarily 33 *consecutive* days — and the Sages therefore decreed 33 days of mourning. However, they left it up to each community to decide which 33 days to choose, resulting in the different practices we have today (see *Igros Moshe* ibid., who uses this explanation to explain certain of the customs, but it would just as well work for all of them). The problem with this answer is: Why should the Sages have done such a thing? Why would the Sages deliberately set up a situation to do harm to *achdus,* the unity of *Klal Yisrael?*

It is surely more than coincidence that the deaths of the disciples all occurred between Pesach and Shavuos. *Sefirah,* the time of counting the *Omer,* commemorates how our ancestors, newly liberated from Egypt, enthusiastically counted the 49 days until they were to receive the Torah at Mt. Sinai at the first Shavuos. Just as they prepared themselves emotionally and spiritually for the great day, Jews in every generation should do the same, using the weeks after Pesach to strengthen enthusiasm for Torah and rid ourselves of every roadblock that stands in the way of our own sincere acceptance of Torah on Shavuos, every year.

Rabbi Akiva's disciples were more than Torah students. They were the very chain of Torah transmission itself, those who would pass the tradition on to the next generation. They were men of great learning, and they undoubtedly excelled in other forms of virtue as well, but in one area they were lacking: "Rabbi Akiva had 12,000 pairs of disciples, from Gevat to Antepares, but they all died in one period because they did not treat one another with respect" (*Yevamos* 62b). We should not be quick to judge. It is possible that the disciples were paragons of courtesy in comparison with us, but Heaven holds disciples of Rabbi Akiva to a higher standard. In any case, measured by the Divine yardstick, they were found wanting.

The Sages wanted to commemorate this, not only to remember the tragedy, but also to remember the spiritual cause of this Heaven-sent plague (if it were not vital for us to know about their spiritual failing in order to learn some lesson from it to apply to ourselves, it would not have been recorded in the Gemara). The Sages therefore instituted the mourning period between Pesach and Shavuos to impress upon us that, to be worthy to learn Torah, we must also learn how to properly act towards one another (parenthetically: Although *Sefirah* mourning is a *minhag*, a "custom," this does not mean it was a spontaneous folk practice; it was almost certainly a decree of the Sages, but a decree they chose to institute with the force of *minhag* and not law — see Rambam's introduction to *Mishnah Torah*).

However, the Sages foresaw a problem: Character flaws and human frailty being what they are, it would be entirely possible for loyal Jews to observe all the mourning practices of *Sefirah*, while completely overlooking any lesson that *Sefirah* is supposed to teach! The prophets long ago warned about fast days that are not accompanied by repentance and good deeds (*Isaiah* 57, Yom Kippur morning Haftarah). *Sefirah* practices are like a string a man ties around his finger to remind him of something. What good is the string, if he never stops to think of what it is meant to signify? (Rav Simcha Zissel, in reference to Chanukah lights).

The Sages therefore instituted 33 days of mourning between Pesach and Shavuos, but they purposely left it to each community to determine *which* 33 to observe. This would lead to a multiplicity of diverse *minhagim*, not by Rabbinic decree, but because each community would end up selecting the option most suited to it, and the different ways are all equally valid. The lesson is thus brought home: We mourn for the disciples ("from Gevat to Antepares" — could that mean to imply that a reason for the lack of respect was that they found it hard to relate to others from different geographical regions, like Ashkenazi/Sephardi relationship difficulties in more recent times?); and the different mourning practices themselves remind us that there is more than one *derech,* more than one authentic approach to serving Hashem, and all approaches sanctioned by the Sages demand our respect.

One of the most beautiful wedding photos I have ever seen is that of a circle of *chaveirim,* friends from the *chasan's* yeshivah, dancing around the *chasan* (bridegroom) at his wedding celebration. The wedding was held two days after Pesach, a time of *Sefirah* mourning when weddings are prohibited for many of us. But this *chasan's* family had always followed the custom that the mourning period begins only a week after Pesach on *Rosh Chodesh Iyar,* so the marriage was permitted. (What if the bride's family had a different custom? Ask your rabbi.)

What makes this photograph so beautiful is that many of the dancers in the circles are young men with 10-days growth of beard. *Their* families followed the custom that mourning practices are the *first* 33 days, and consequently they had not shaved since before Pesach. *But they were all at the wedding.* They were to some extent in mourning, but nevertheless they were dancing, and their unshaven cheeks added an extra dimension to the *simchah;* the knowledge that even when we are different, all who unite to keep the Torah rejoice together. At the foot of the mountain, each of us stands at a different place; but we come closer together as we climb up towards the peak, and we all give encouragement to each other as we ascend.

SKETCH FROM AFAR: THE CONVERT

Five books are known as *Megillos: Esther, Song of Songs, Ruth, Lamentations and Ecclesiastes*. Each *Megillah* is read on the special day which parallels that book's central theme, with *Megillas Esther* read on Purim, the lamentations of *Eichah* on Tishah B'Av, and so on. The connection between each *Megillah* and its day is not difficult to discern, with one exception.

On Shavuos, when we recall the giving of the Torah at Mt. Sinai, we read the Book of *Ruth*. The story of Ruth appears to be totally unrelated to the Yom Tov of Shavuos or the experience at Sinai, and the main character is not from Israel but is a righteous convert from the pagan nation of Moav. What is this story doing in our Shavuos *Machzor*?

A traditional answer is that we read the *Megillah* because it mentions the lineage of *David Hamelech, King David,* who was born and who died on Shavuos, and Ruth was King David's great-grandmother. But it seems this is no more than a partial explanation, because Shavuos itself is not directly connected with King David, and to mention him it would have sufficed to read the *Megillah's* concluding paragraph where his name appears. Why do we need Ruth's entire life story, why "the whole *Megillah*"?

Aside from asking how Ruth is part of Shavuos, we can also ask: How is Ruth part of the Torah as a whole? Her story is different from all other books. The 24 volumes of *Tanach*, all of Scriptures, are chronicles of the Jewish nation and its leaders. *Tanach* contains no books of biography of private individuals, ordinary people, except for the Book of *Ruth*. What is in her book that is so important that it must be included in the *Tanach*, forever?

Each Yom Tov has its own special mitzvos, and on most Yamim Tovim we symbolically reenact what occurred at the original historical event. We recall the Egyptian Exodus with matzah and *maror*, we recall Divine protection in the Wilderness by sitting in a *succah*, and we relive the thanksgiving celebration of Jews in ancient Persia by indulging on Purim in thanksgiving celebrations of our own. The Torah commands us to relive the experiences of the past, to educate us in the great lessons the past has to teach.

Delving more deeply, teachers of the Kabbalah tell us that on Yom Tov, the Divine Spirit that was manifest at the original Pesach and Succos returns, and our mitzvah reenactment of those days helps us bring something of that Spirit into ourselves. But, on whatever level we understand the reason for reliving history, why is Shavuos so very different? It is virtually the only major holiday without any tangible mitzvah symbol. No matzah, no *succah*, no *shofar* (blintzes don't count) — why is Shavuos so lacking in symbolism?

The answer is: Shavuos commemorates the high point of all history; the day, more than 33 centuries ago, when Israel stood at the foot of Mt. Sinai and accepted a commitment to do Hashem's Will, as expressed in His eternal Torah.

One cannot relive that experience by standing at a mountain in the Catskills. The only act for us to perform on Shavuos is to re-create our ancestors accepting the Torah, by accepting the Torah ourselves, here and now. Shavuos is the day for us to decide that we too want the Divine closeness, we too need Hashem's guidance, and we too proclaim *Naaseh v'nishma*, we will keep mitzvos and study them to make them an integral part of our souls. That is Shavuos, a single day (in *Eretz Yisrael*; two days elsewhere) for us to personally accept the entire Torah.

However, there is a problem: If the mitzvah is to accept the Torah, then it must be that we are looking from the perspective of men and women who have not yet accepted. If your Torah commitment is already total, then there is nothing left for you to do on Shavuos except eat blintzes. Our Shavuos mitzvah is to accept whatever Torah we have not yet accepted; and, paradoxically, the less observant a Jew is, the more he or she needs to accept and the more meaningful Shavuos becomes.

At the same time, if the mitzvah is to take on a new commitment which until now I did not have, the Torah is not going to just say "Abracadabra, transform your life." If, for whatever reason, the Torah is presently only 50 percent of my life, or only 5 percent or no percent, and if Shavuos demands radical change, then the Torah must provide some method, some system for a sincere person to be able to spiritually improve.

Rambam (Maimonides) wrote in his *Mishneh Torah*, in the *halachos* of *geirus* (laws of conversion to Judaism): "At Sinai, Israel entered the covenant with G-d by means of three acts, circumcision, ritual immersion and sacrificial offering... So too for all generations, if a non-Jew desires to enter the covenant and he accepts the yoke of the Torah, he too requires these three things, circumcision, ritual immersion and sacrificial offering." *Rambam* is pointing out that there exists a direct link: The procedure for today's converts follows that of our national experience at Sinai, because both are engaged in the same enterprise, both are accepting the Torah and entering the covenant with G-d.

To obtain a picture of what happened at Sinai to the Jewish nation as a whole, we learn *Chumash*. But to discover how each of us as individuals today can bring ourselves to an acceptance of Torah this Shavuos, we must examine the story of a sincere individual convert, someone who accepted the Torah on her own. Sinai was the conversion to Judaism of the entire nation; our mitzvah today is for each of us to make an effort to reconvert ourselves.

To teach us how, *Tanach* devotes an entire volume to the story of one person who did it, perhaps the greatest convert of all: the *Megillah* of *Ruth*. We need this narrative, whose subject is not the whole nation and not the nation's king, but an ordinary (though extraordinarily righteous) person like ourselves. And we read it on Shavuos to serve as a guide, to help reconvert to Judaism ordinary people, like ourselves.

Examine the story. A Jewish woman named Naomi moved from *Eretz Yisrael* to Moav, together with her husband and two sons. The husband dies. The sons marry women from Moav, named Ruth and Orpah. Then the sons die. Naomi, in dire poverty, returns to *Eretz Yisrael*, and her two daughters-in-law express their loyalty by insisting they will accompany her.

Naomi tells them it is foolish for young women to doom themselves to widowhood and destitution in a foreign land, and she urges them to return to their own families. Orpah says a tearful goodbye. But Ruth replies, in one of the most famous passages in all *Tanach*:

"*Al tifge'i vi,* Do not entreat me to leave you. For wherever you go, I will go. Where you lodge, I will lodge. Your people are my people. Your G-d is my G-d. Where you die, I will die, and there I will be buried. I swear by Hashem, that only death will separate me from you."

Words in *Tanach* can be understood on several levels, but we must begin with the plain meaning. In the plain meaning of these verses, we discover what was Ruth's motivation to become a Jew. "Do not entreat me to leave you. For wherever you go, I will go." This seems to imply that Ruth's motive was her personal devotion to Naomi, "Do not entreat me to leave you." Her commitment to Naomi brings her to say, "Your people are my people," and that commitment to the nation leads her to say, "Your G-d is my G-d." There are three distinct steps: Ruth's attachment to Naomi, to Naomi's people, and finally to Naomi's G-d. And that creates a problem.

It creates a problem, because it is a well-known *halachah* that conversion candidates with ulterior motives are not to be accepted. If a non-Jew tells the Rabbis, "Convert me, so that I can marry a nice Jewish doctor," the Rabbinic answer is an unequivocal "No!" Yet here, in the classic case of *geirus*, the case the Talmud uses as a source for *halachah* in *geirus*, here it seems Ruth's only goal was to follow Naomi, and for that reason alone she converts!

But the explanation here is that it is not so. Unlike the case of the non-Jew who seeks conversion in order to marry a Jew, Ruth did not have to become Jewish to remain with Naomi. Ruth could have simply accepted the seven Noahide mitzvos of universal morality, and in her status as a righteous gentile she could have remained on excellent terms with Naomi and all Israel.

The real meaning of the *Megillah* is that Ruth said: I want to follow Naomi, there is something in this person that inspires. Then Ruth realizes: The inspiration is not merely Naomi's personality. It's her spirituality, it is Naomi's Jewishness that draws me to her, and Ruth says: Not only will I follow you, but I want to be part of the nation that produced you, "your people are my people."

But after Ruth attains this insight, that her love for Naomi is really a love for the goodness of the people of Israel, Ruth then moves on to a higher level. She comes to perceive that Jewish uniqueness is not a mere ethnic quality, that Jews are attractive in the same way that some people are attracted to the British or the French. Instead, she now perceives that the beauty of Naomi's life, which she has come to realize is the beauty of Jewish life, is actually the beauty of Torah; and all Jewish greatness lies in the unique relationship of the Jewish people with Hashem.

First, Ruth says, "Wherever you go, I will go." Then she comprehends that her feeling means something more: "Your people are mine." Finally, she arrives at the truth, that what she really seeks is "your G-d is my G-d"; and Ruth converts not for Naomi, and not for Naomi's people, but for Naomi's G-d.

This is an important lesson, especially for parents and educators. In choosing fundamental values and a way of life, real people do not use philosophy texts or mathematical formulae. Instead, you meet someone you admire, a parent or teacher or peer who serves as a role model, and from your attraction to the person you become attracted to that person's way of life. It is not that we are simple-minded or easily fooled. It is that one cannot appreciate ideology in the abstract; one cannot want to be a Jew until one has seen what an authentic Jew looks like.

The great teacher Rav Simchah Zissel Ziv once said: Charles Darwin claimed that human beings descend from apes. It is understandable that Darwin should have thought so, because Darwin never saw Rav Yisrael Salanter. But he, Rav Simcha Zissel, did see Rav Yisrael Salanter, so he knows with absolute certainty: The origin of humanity is Divine.

The reason most Jews today do not keep Shabbos is not intellectual error or cultural conflict. It is only because almost all their peers and role models are ignorant of Shabbos, because they themselves never had the chance to meet the Baal Shem Tov or the Vilna Gaon, and they have never even seen the best of Torah living today.

I once witnessed an argument between two students in a yeshivah dormitory, where one of two available beds was much more comfortable than the other, and each student was insistent that the OTHER student take the better bed. I also remember how the recent arrival down the hall had no pillow, and my roommate gave the new boy his own pillow, telling him that he had an extra one (yes, my roommate lied, and I have never let him forget it). You need not be a scholar to recognize that in such a yeshivah, there are things worth learning.

We become elevated through contact with elevated human beings, and the best education for every Jew is to hang out with the right people, until something rubs off on us that we say: Your people are the kind of people I wish to be, and your G-d is the One I wish to make my own. That is one fundamental lesson from Ruth, to find righteous people to admire, and learn from them to admire righteousness itself.

Before accepting candidates for *geirus* (conversion), we are required by *halachah* to give them some idea of the obligations of the Torah, by mentioning to them several mitzvos as examples. Try to picture in your mind, if a sincere non–Jew asked you for a brief description of Judaism, which commandments would you choose to mention? Put this book down and make a mental list of three or four representative mitzvos, right now. (Do it! Really. I don't mind waiting for you.)

The Sages of the Gemara had a tradition of the list of mitzvos Naomi chose to tell Ruth. Naomi put six items on her list. Here they are, in the order in which she said them:

#1. *Techumim*, the prohibition against walking outside the city beyond a certain point on Shabbos.

#2. *Yichud*, the prohibition against a man and woman who are not husband and wife being alone together in a secluded place.

#3. There are 613 Biblical commandments.

#4. Idolatry is forbidden.

#5. Jewish courts have the authority to impose four types of capital punishment.

#6. Executed Jewish criminals are buried in two different cemeteries, depending on the severity of their crime.

Now, compare your list with Naomi's. How many items are the same? Probably none, unless you included the prohibition against worshipping idols. But to introduce mitzvah obligations with the laws of Shabbos travel, male-female seclusion, 613 commandments, idolatry, four types of death and two types of burial — what is Naomi getting at?

For us to accept the Torah with a true commitment, it is not enough to know a handful of laws, not even a large handful. We must also have some comprehension of what the structure of Torah is all about, what is the sacred building which all the mitzvah building-blocks create. Naomi chose her specific examples because each one of them illustrates a general

Torah principle, a principle each of us needs to grasp even to-day. The principles are:

#1. *Techumim*, the prohibition against walking outside the city beyond a certain point on Shabbos. We must begin by coming to understand that the Creator has set boundaries, limits on human behavior. Most people like to have Hashem around for special occasions like weddings and *bar mitzvahs*, but in daily life they themselves want to be the gods, and whatever they choose goes. But to enter the covenant of the Torah, for Hashem to place His Name upon us and be bound together with us, the first prerequisite for us is to accept that He alone is the Master, and we must follow His Plan instead of our own.

#2. *Yichud*, the prohibition against a man and woman who are not husband and wife being alone together in a secluded place. This is a precautionary measure, to avoid circum-stances that might possibly lead to wrongdoing. *Halachah* is filled with such precautions, and many people think it extreme that the *halachah* is so extraordinarily strict. But how much caution is appropriate depends on the value of the thing you wish to protect.

Some years ago, it was discovered that a popular brand of bottled water contained a minute trace of a chemical which, it was estimated, would increase the consumer's chances of getting cancer by (literally) one in a million. ALL bottles of that brand were removed from the market, and the product itself was reformulated. But why? To be so fanatically extreme, because of danger to one in a million? But even if the gov-ernment did not demand the product's removal, consumer rejection would have compelled it, because we refuse to take chances with our lives and the lives of our children.

So too with Yiddishkeit. If Torah is merely a cultural tradi-tion, like playing bagpipes or wearing a dashiki, then one may certainly choose not to pay too high a price for continuing to enjoy those pleasures. But if "*ki heim chayeinu*," if the Torah is our life and the life of our children, then we take no chances. Converts must accept all the precautionary measures as well, and comprehending the necessity of doing so is part of their comprehending the nature of the Torah they are coming to accept.

#3. There are 613 Biblical commandments. A sociologist in the 1960s made a survey to try to determine how many Orthodox Jews there are in the United States, but from the beginning he was faced with a problem: How does one define "Orthodox"? After much thought, the pollster's answer was that true Orthodoxy is contingent upon *Taharas Hamishpachah*, whether husband and wife observe the mitzvah of *mikveh* and family purity. Why is *Taharas Hamishpachah* the deciding factor?

The sociologist explained: A non-Orthodox couple cannot imagine that the Torah would dare to tell them how to act in their most private relationship. But an Orthodox couple cannot imagine that the Torah would refrain from telling them how to act! If Torah is the guide to living, then it applies to every sphere of human activity; and Naomi brought home the point by noting that there are literally hundreds of Biblical mitzvos, 613, plus countless more instituted by the Sages.

#4. Idolatry is forbidden. Idolatry is the belief that there exists a force with true power other than Hashem, and that false belief takes many forms besides bowing to sticks and stones. I remember from my childhood years in Massachusetts how mitzvah-observant Jews put their faith in Hashem and in Senator Kennedy, just as their parents had relied on Hashem and President Roosevelt, and not necessarily in that order. With faith in our Jewish organizations, in our political clout, and faith in our own skills and intelligence and earning power, are we not like the British royal family whose coat of arms reads (in French): "The Lord — and My Right Arm"?

Surely we must support our friends in politics, and we must use the skills Hashem gave us, and sometimes we must even use a strong right arm, because that use is itself the Will of Hashem. But if we assign to them an independent importance, a feeling on an intellectual or an emotional level that we must have them, then our focus is not solely on Hashem, and Ruth (and we) must be guided to recognize the full implications of "*Hashem Echad*, Hashem is the One and Only."

#5. Jewish courts have the authority to impose four types of capital punishment. In general, we need to learn more in order to properly understand the place of punishment in the Torah system (e.g., is it chiefly for the good of society or of the transgressor himself, serving the function of retribution/atonement/deterrent, etc.). But Naomi's basic point is: Judaism is not a hobby, like playing tennis or canasta. Torah is the world in which a Jew lives, and its laws are like laws of nature. Try to break natural laws, go skydiving without a parachute, and there are consequences. To get where she wishes to go, Ruth must be aware: Our actions do make a difference, and there is a judgment that is exact.

#6. Executed Jewish criminals are buried in two different cemeteries, depending on the severity of their crime. We need to know this, because we need to know that what we do with our days lives on, affecting us tomorrow and the day after and even after death. All of creation was made for each one of us; and our every act, even our every thought, good or bad, shapes our destiny, forever.

To sum up, we learn from Ruth a path to spiritual motivation: Association with true Torah people leads a sincere person to an appreciation for true Torah values. And we also learn from Ruth the process of personal Torah acceptance: first, a commitment to living within Divinely ordained limits; then, the need to take precautions; the bringing of Torah into all areas of our lives; rejection of all man-made gods; acceptance of responsibility for our own acts; and recognition that the impact of our acts is eternal.

But even if we take the lessons to heart and apply them, to develop personal motivation and personal commitment, they are still not enough, because there is no guarantee that the commitment will last. I feel inspired today, but what if tomorrow I feel bored or depressed or just plain lazy? Once I have become motivated to accept the fullness of Torah for myself, what will keep me going when the going gets rough?

Again, we find the answer in the *Megillah*. Ruth has just finished her eternally inspiring affirmation of "wherever you go, I will go," etc. What was its effect of Naomi? "*Vateire ki misametzes*, Naomi saw" — NOT that Ruth was sincerely motivated, and not that Ruth was totally committed, but that she was *misametzes*, "that she was determined." Ruth was determined to follow Naomi and Naomi's way of life, persistent in her refusal to give up; *vatechdal* — then Naomi accepted her.

The *Shulchan Aruch* commands us to attempt to dissuade the potential convert. We are to tell them that being Jewish is difficult, and keeping mitzvos is a fearsome responsibility. If, after all our efforts, they keep coming back, if they refuse to give up, then we know that this is someone who can live the Torah. *Misametzes*, a determination to persist — that is the test.

In the heyday of the great Slabodka Yeshivah, part of the entrance exam was that Rav Nosson Zvi Finkel (the "Alter from Slabodka") would tell the applicant that there was no more room for new students. The young man's reaction would determine whether or not he would be accepted.

In a similar case, a young woman once applied to the Jewish Teacher's Training College in Gateshead, England (the "Gateshead Sem"), and the principal, Mr. Kohn, told her truthfully that every seat in the classroom was already filled. She replied: "I'm not demanding a seat. If necessary, I'll stand in the hallway, as long as I can have the opportunity to listen in." She was accepted, and with Hashem's help they found her a seat as well.

A student once asked the great Rav Shlomo Heiman, Rosh Hayeshivah of Mesivta Torah Vodaas, what he should do when he has no desire for Torah learning. Rav Heiman replied: "Then learn, without desire." There will always be difficulties, and the classic *Mesillas Yesharim* writes that life's purpose is "to work, to persist, and to withstand temptation." Our task is to not surrender; to persist a bit more to continue doing however much or little we can, until the time comes that Heaven will bless us with success.

And if we do persist, it is astonishing how much difference the extra effort can make. Naomi's other daughter-in-law,

Orpah, also wished to accompany her, but when Naomi urged her to return home, Orpah left. She remarried, and became famous for one of her descendants named Golias, the giant Goliath who sought to enslave Israel, and who was finally slain by his distant cousin David.

Ruth, by persisting a bit longer, remained with Naomi and with Naomi's people. Ruth also remarried, but her great-grandson was King David, and another of her descendants will be *Melech Hamashiach*, the Messianic king.

And this is why we read the *Megillah*, the story of Ruth, on Shavuos: to teach us of the need to get close to the best Jews we can find; to recognize the need for limits; safeguards; to-tal mitzvah involvement; rejection of idolatry; acceptance of responsibility; a sense of eternity; and unshakeable persis-tence. By learning Ruth's lessons, we can make use of the *Megillah* and of Shavuos to re-convert ourselves to Judaism; and to gain for ourselves a *zechus*, a merit, to be able to wel-come Ruth's descendant the *Mashiach*, and teach these lessons to all the world.

SUCCOS AND SHEMINI ATZERES

TEMPORARY DWELLINGS

The *halachah* is that a *succah* may not be higher than 20 *amos*, which is about 38 feet. The Gemara in *Succah* 2a gives the reason: "The Torah said, for all seven days go out from the permanent dwelling and reside in a temporary dwelling. Under 20 *amos* high, one can build a temporary dwelling; above 20 *amos*, one does not build a temporary dwelling, but a permanent dwelling." We see here that one of the *succah's* defining characteristics is that it is *diras arai*, a temporary dwelling. Buildings higher than 20 *amos* require solid structural support so that they will not collapse, and are therefore not considered temporary, and not kosher as *succos*.

The Gemara then asks: What about a *succah* of normal height, with kosher *s'chach* (material that is permissible for use as a *succah* roof), but with *mechitzos shel barzel*, walls of iron? Do solid, permanent walls also invalidate the *succah*? The Gemara says no, a solid iron *succah* is permitted. What's the difference between an overly high *succah* and a metal *succah*?

The Gemara explains: A height less than 20 *amos* is suitable for a temporary dwelling, and therefore even if he made his *succah* a permanent metal structure it is permitted. But higher than 20 *amos*, since that height is suitable only for permanent buildings, the *succah* is not valid.

This is very strange. If the essence of a *succah* is that it is a temporary dwelling, and therefore it cannot be too high, why does it suffice for the *succah* to be of a temporary height if the *succah* itself is a permanent metal structure?

Rosh Hashanah and Yom Kippur are days spent in *shul*, and they are days of spiritual elevation. But most of us do not live our lives inside a *shul*. Most of our lives are spent at home, at work, and in places where spiritual values do not take center stage. How do we retain the inspiration of Rosh Hashanah and Yom Kippur and package it, to be able to use it in daily life? For this, right after Yom Kippur, the Torah gives us the Yom Tov of Succos.

The central Succos experience does not take place in *shul* but in the *succah*, a dwelling place, a symbol that we wish to sanctify the places where we eat and drink and live our daily lives. The *succah* is the place to take the Yom Kippur inspiration and try to experience some of it while we enjoy a good meal, together with family and friends. And the theme of the *succah* is that we *do* live in the material world, but it is a *diras arai*, a dwelling that is temporary.

Throughout history, the most prominent symbol of a wealthy man was his palatial home. Even the poor man can think that his home is his castle, it's *his*; and he may come to believe that what you *own* defines who you *are*.

Succos come to remind us that this is not true. Everything we own is only on loan to us, temporary; 50, 60 or 80 years and then it is gone. What we attained on Yom Kippur, *teshuvah*, *tefillah*, *tzedakah*, is permanent, and that is who we are. So on Succos Hashem tells us to leave our so-called permanent dwelling for a temporary dwelling, to teach us to view all our possessions in proper perspective.

This leads to the question: What *is* the proper perspective? Should we completely negate the idea of material possessions? Is it a Jewish ideal to give away all our property, and live in poverty in a thatched-roof hut all year round? That is not so. The Torah is replete with examples of the righteous being blessed with wealth, and wealth and possessions are almost always seen as blessings (in our tradition we do find sources indicating that it is easier to be a poor *tzaddik* than a rich *tzaddik*; still, if you have the choice, a wealthy *tzaddik* has the means which enable him to accomplish more in other areas).

The Mishnah (*Avos* 6:4) tells us, "*Kach hi darchah shel Torah*, this is the way of Torah: Eat bread with salt, drink water in small measure, sleep on the ground, live a life of deprivation — but toil in Torah-study. If you do this, you will be happy, and it will be good for you." Nowhere else in our tradition do we find that we are to sleep on the ground instead of a bed, and nowhere else do we find that our diet should be restricted to bread and water; yet here it says that this is the way of Torah, and also the way to be happy.

But the meaning is: One Shabbos we were giving out candy to our little boys, and our 2–year–old received a red lollipop. Normally, he would have been very happy with this, except that it happened that his 5–year–old brother received a *green* lollipop, so the 2–year–old was miserable. On the other hand, to the 7–year–old it made no difference which color he received, and the 16–year–old does not care for lollipops at all.

There is nothing improper with enjoying a Shabbos treat of a tasty lollipop. But if you find that you *must* have the lollipop, and you must have it just so, in one particular color and flavor, then you are opening yourself up to a life of misery.

Another (unfortunately, not uncommon) example: Picture two men in *shul*, Reuven and Shimon, both of whom enjoy being called up to the Torah to receive an *aliyah*. If Reuven does not receive an *aliyah*, it does not disturb him; but if Shimon does not get the *aliyah* he desires, when he desires, his morning is ruined, and he may walk out of the *shul* in a huff.

The general rule is: The more things you *need* to be happy, the more vulnerable you are to misery when those things are absent. That is why the Rosh Yeshivah of Torah Vodaas, Rav Yaakov Kamenetzky *z"l*, never ate ice cream. He said that growing up in Russia, he never had tasted ice cream. Now in America, at his advanced age, should he begin developing a craving for it? (heard from Rabbi Eliyahu Goldschmidt). We Americans would say, "A new taste sensation? Sure! How can you deprive yourself?" But the wise man or woman knows that every additional desire, whatever you come to salivate over, is one more thing you come to need, and it enslaves you.

And this is the meaning of the Mishnah in *Avos*. There is nothing wrong with eating well and sleeping in luxury. But the way of Torah is to train yourself so that such things are not important. To strive for the ideal that you can be satisfied with bread and salt and a little water, and a place on the floor to sleep. If you can live that way — you do not have to, but if you *can* —if you can live on the barest minimum and toil in Torah, then you are the happy person, in this world and the next (based on the writing of Rav Nachum Zev Ziv of Kelm).

And a source for this idea in the Mishnah is the mitzvah of *succah*. It is permissible to build a *succah* with permanent walls of brick or iron, or even walls of silver and gold. But the *succah* must be low enough that the structure *could* be temporary, that the limited height of our living space does not *have* to be solid. That is the true goal, to enjoy our material possessions while at the same time feeling that we do not need them, because material possessions are not why we're here. Control the use of your possessions, don't let your possessions control you.

The goal is liberation: to feel that our happiness is not dependent upon any external things, and that we need not fear the loss of any external thing.

And perhaps this is part of the idea of Succos being called *zman simchaseinu*, the time of our rejoicing. When external circumstances cease to control us, and we see the world as a temporary dwelling, that is what allows us to focus on what is truly important, where we directed our thoughts on Rosh Hashanah and Yom Kippur. To know that our relationship with Hashem is the only thing that is permanent, and that it is a relationship we take with us wherever we go, gives us a sense of enduring *simchah*, in every dwelling we enter, and in everything we do.

BIG JOYS,
LITTLE JOYS

We do not know the reason for every mitzvah, and reasons are not always necessary for us to know. The mitzvah of *succah* is different, in that the Torah not only gives a reason, but also (according to *Bach, Orach Chaim* 625) commands us to think of that reason when we are in the *succah*: "*Lemaan yeidu doroseichem*, that all your generations should know" how Hashem protected us in the Wilderness for 40 years, and He continues to protect us today.

Isn't it odd that the symbol of Divine protection is a fragile, rickety *succah*, three or four walls with some sticks or branches of *s'chach* on top? Why not symbolize Divine protection by building a miniature fortress, stone walls and a tower of strength to proclaim the might of Hashem? Besides being a more impressive reminder, would that not be a truer expression of our gratitude for the Divine protection that guides our lives?

Every Yom Tov includes a mitzvah of rejoicing, but Succos joy, "*zman simchaseinu*, the time of our rejoicing," is the greatest of all. What is the high point of this rejoicing? The Mishnah says that the greatest rejoicing occurred on Succos in the *Beis Hamikdash*, when our ancestors gave thanks to Hashem with an offering of water on the *mizbei'ach*, the altar. There was singing and dancing led by the greatest Sages, all part of thanking Hashem for the life-giving blessing of water.

The *mizbei'ach* was a place for many other offerings as well; baked goods and wine and meat, offerings which afford much greater *simchah* than plain water. So why is it that the greatest celebration was reserved for H_2O?

Perhaps the answer is: The Torah is teaching us how to *become* happy, the way to attain the state of true *simchas Yom Tov*. And that way is: In order to appreciate the blessing of luxuries, we must first learn to appreciate the blessing of basic necessities.

There are many stories of *tzaddikim* who ate nothing but bread and water. But I once heard from Rav Avigdor Miller, that when the *tzaddik* made a *brachah* over his crust of bread, and he said, "*Baruch ata Hashem*, the source of this blessed bread is You, Hashem"; *Elokeinu Melech Haolam*, Sovereign of the world Who is our G-d, Who cares for each one of us"; "*hamotzi lechem min ha'aretz*, Who miraculously takes bread out of the ground, tasty nutrition from dirt!" — that *tzaddik* savored his crust of bread with a *simchah* we will never know.

Appreciate the blessing of bread. Celebrate the great gift of water. Learn to feel the ecstasy in the basics. And then you can come to truly enjoy the meat and the wine and everything else.

The *succah* is a three-dimensional thank-you note to Hashem for protecting us, in ancient times and today. How often do we complain that something in our home is inconvenient, or in need of repair, or is not as splendid as that of our neighbors?

The *succah* reminds us: Give thanks for the exquisite joy that Hashem has blessed you with four walls and a roof over your head, even if it is only a roof of *s'chach*. Thousands of people live on the streets of India (and more than a few on the streets of America) without any shelter at all. First learn to savor the pleasure of having the one-room shelter of a *succah*, and *then* you will be able to rejoice in the palatial home you reside in all year round.

There is the beautiful joy of food and drink, beginning with water. There is the joyous beauty of a home, beginning with a *succah*. And there is the joy of beauty itself, the happiness we experience from the aesthetic dimension which is part of human life. The Torah speaks of beauty many times, from the "glory and splendor" ("*lechavod ul'sifares*," Exodus 28:2) of the Kohen's vestments to the Sages' lamenting that handsome men and woman must die ("*hai shufra d'vali b'afra*," *Berachos* 5b and elsewhere) to their instituting a special *berachah* to say when seeing beautiful things (*Orach Chaim* 225:10). And on Succos, as part of our joyous thanksgiving, the Torah commands us to rejoice before Hashem with a thing of beauty, "*pri eitz hadar*," the fruit of beauty which we call an *esrog*.

Is an *esrog*, or an esrog tree, so beautiful? (True, the price of a piece of art and the price of an *esrog* are comparable, but we seldom think of *esrogim* as fine art.) But the Torah says it is beautiful, and it is, with an aesthetic value all its own. An *esrog* is not the Mona Lisa. But if we focus on it, simply to enjoy its color and symmetry and bouquet and the exquisite feel of the most beautiful fruit in *Eretz Yisrael*, we too can come to feel the joy of *pri eitz hadar*.

Along with the *esrog* we are to take *hadassim*, which the Torah calls *anaf eitz avos*, a bracelet of intertwined leaves; *aravos*, called *arvei nachal*, willows of the brook, calling to mind a willow tree overhanging a tranquil country stream; and a *lulav*, called *kapos temarim*, literally a palm, a hand, offering us its clusters of dates.

We are commanded to take these plants "*usemachtem lifnei Hashem*," rejoice with them before Hashem. That joy includes all the symbolism taught by the Sages, that *lulav* and *esrog* represent different kinds of Jews, and different parts of the body, all joining together for the mitzvah. But even without the symbolism, even for the simple Jew who knows only the simple meaning of the words, the mitzvah is given to us to enjoy the physical beauty of the here and now, rejoicing with the mitzvos of beauty which are given to all of us to share.

Today, with sportscars, camcorders, computers and all sorts of electronic toys to entertain us, one would expect that our joys would be much greater than those of our grandparents. But it is not so. Too much sugar desensitizes the palate, and we cannot enjoy the finer things when our senses are overwhelmed by the noise of extravaganza. The pounding of rock music (even "Jewish" rock music) makes it harder to appreciate a subtle melody line, and the patter of the comedian deadens our ability to appreciate true wit.

The evening of the 1964 American presidential election, one of the national television networks sponsored a 20-minute discussion by partisans of the rival candidates, an informal debate between intelligent, articulate noncelebrities. For the 1976 elections the debaters were invited back for a rematch, but the producers would allow them only seven minutes of discussion instead of 20; because research indicated that in the intervening 12 years, the American public had lost the ability to concentrate more than 420 seconds at a stretch (I have not checked the more recent figures, because I'm afraid to find out). Excess of every sort destroys our ability to enjoy the basic, which ultimately destroys every available joy.

An American fighter pilot was once lost in the Pacific Ocean, stranded on a life raft for 26 days. When he was finally rescued, he was asked if he had learned anything from his ordeal. He replied: "I learned that if you have enough to eat, and all the fresh water you need to drink, then you should never, every worry about anything."

Succos is a time for *simchah*. The *simchah* that Hashem gives us shelter, and water, and beauties of nature, and so much more. The *halachah* is to drink wine on Yom Tov, and that a husband should buy new clothing for his wife. The outcome is a beautiful family in a beautiful home, rejoicing together with beautiful Jews everywhere in *zman simchaseinu*, the time of rejoicing for all the blessings of Hashem's beautiful world, a world in which the greatest beauty is the blessing of being alive.

CLOUD COVER

The *succah* is one of the few mitzvos where the Torah tells us to think about the reason for the mitzvah while performing it: "*Lemaan yeidu doroseichem*, that all your generations should know that I, Hashem, caused the Children of Israel to dwell in *succos*." Since we are commanded to think about this, it is beneficial to know what these ancient *succos* were, what manner of *succah* did the Creator make for us.

One opinion in the Gemara is *succos mamash*, that when we left Egypt 3300 years ago Hashem provided us with building materials to construct *succos* for shelter. One problem with that interpretation is that the Torah often mentions our fathers living in the Wilderness in tents, not *succos*. But there is also a second opinion, more generally accepted, that our *succah* today is to commemorate the *ananei kavod*, the clouds of the Divine Presence which protected us for 40 years.

The Torah says that Hashem placed a pillar of cloud to lead us through the desert, and the Sages add that this cloud surrounded us from all sides to shield us from inclement weather and wild animals, a total protection plan in a climate-controlled environment. The word "*succah*" literally means a cover, and our *succah* recalls that miraculous cloud cover that accompanied us for 40 years.

However, this interpretation also has its problems. If we are commemorating Heavenly protection, it would seem that the halachah should require us to build a *succah* that protects, one which is waterproof and insectproof. But the halachah is exactly the opposite, that a *succah* must be fragile and it must let in the rain, *diras arai*, a temporary dwelling.

A second problem: The Divine cloud cover protected us from all sides. But the *halachah* is that a *succah* requires only three walls, not four, and the essence of the *succah*, the cover of *s'chach*, is placed only on top. So the lesson the *succah* comes to teach must be something more than Divine protection; clearly the accent is on something else.

Ideally, the *succah* should serve as a reminder that Hashem protects us, that He is all-powerful, and we sit back in relaxed tranquility, knowing we are completely safe in His Hands. If you are that holy a person to be so inspired by the *succah*, you are a member of a very select group of *tzaddikim* (one almost wonders if such a person even has need of a *succah* in the first place). What about the rest of us? What about simple Jews with personal concerns and anxieties, Jews who possess *emunah* (faith) but whose *emunah* is not so powerful that it transcends all the worries of daily living?

For us, the *halachah* says: Focus on the *s'chach*, which recalls only one part of the Divine cloud, the part above; the Torah says this part of the cloud served as an indicator that it was time to travel.

The people of Israel were encamped in the Wilderness, for days or weeks (sometimes months or years) at a stretch. Suddenly, the cloud overhead began to move — time to go! We asked ourselves, "Where are we going?" "We don't know." "How long is the trip?" "Don't know." "Will the next camp be an overnight stop, or an extended stay?" "No way to tell."

It was not easy. The insecurity of not being able to make plans, the feeling that you could never settle down, *Ramban* writes, was almost a kind of mental torture. But one thing we knew: We were traveling *al pi Hashem,* Hashem is guiding us. Most of us are not relaxed. We feel unsettled and nervous. But Hashem knows the way, and in the end, He will get us where we need to go.

There is a level of powerful faith called *bitachon,* complete serenity. But for those of us who do not possess that power, we sit in the *succah,* a fragile shelter, and we look at the *s'chach;* a few drops of rain, a couple of mosquitoes. And we say to ourselves:

"I have my worries. I don't have the *tzaddik's* peace of mind. But just as my ancestors knew, when the cloud began to move, that it would be rough, but Hashem would get them through; in my case, too, the *succah* reminds me that frail as the structure of my life may be, whatever the bumps in the road, it may be rough, but in the end Hashem will get me through.

"To say it will all turn out great? I'm not at that high a spiritual level. But to say it will all turn out *right,* the way He wants it? That much the *succah* can teach, even me."

This explanation might also help to answer the famous question of why the Yom Tov of Succos is celebrated in the month of Tishrei. The events the Yom Tov commemorates took place all year round for 40 years, and the clouds first appeared after the Exodus in the month of Nissan, so why is Succos in Tishrei?

The answer is that Tishrei is the time when the annual harvest has finally been gathered in, when people are most relaxed knowing that the crops are safely stored away. We are also at ease after passing through the day of forgiveness, on Yom Kippur.

We cannot rationally deal with anxiety in a state of tension (which is why the psychiatrist keeps a couch in his office, for the patient to relax on or for himself). But in Tishrei, at our most comfortable time (when even the kids are back in school!), Tishrei is when we can honestly face ourselves, our difficulties, and our goals for the coming year. Without hiding our fears, without pretending a confidence we may not feel, in Tishrei we can enter the *succah* and know that we are not alone. Hashem is leading the way; and if we keep going in His direction we will end up, not necessarily where we had hoped to be, but in the place that for us is indeed the promised land.

LEARNING TO WAIT

On Rosh Hashanah and Yom Kippur, Jews do *teshuvah*, they repent from their sins, and resolve to make this year a better one than the last. On Rosh Hashanah and Yom Kippur, Jews also *daven*, asking Hashem to make this a better year, *shanah tovah umesukah*, a year of sweetness and good. But the sincerest resolutions and the most heartfelt prayers are not enough, if there is no follow-through after Yom Kippur ends.

Talmud Yerushalmi (the Jerusalem Talmud) relates a parable: A man needed royal assistance, and he knocked on the gates of the king's palace. The king himself rose from his throne to personally let the man in; but in the few seconds it took for the king to reach the door, the man got tired of waiting and walked away, losing his great opportunity.

Our Yom Kippur prayers, and the striking our hearts during *vidui* (the prayer of confession), are a knocking at the gates of Heaven. Yom Kippur ends, we sound the *shofar* one last time, Hashem opens the door — and all too often He finds no one there, we have already walked away. That is one reason why Yom Kippur is so quickly followed by Succos, a Yom Tov which is an opportunity for us to show that Yom Kippur did have meaning, that we seek out more mitzvos (*succah*, *lulav*, *hoshanos*) to follow through on our Yom Kippur resolutions to be good.

But just as doing mitzvos is a follow-up to our resolutions to be better people, there should also be some follow-up to our prayers for a sweet year. When the King opens the door with a smile, is there something special we should say or do?

One answer is that we know Succos is called *zman simchaseinu*, the time of our rejoicing. And one reason to rejoice is in order to show our desire that the apple and honey and all the blessings of a sweet new year were not only for two days of Rosh Hashanah, but we want the sweetness and the joy to continue year round. A second follow-up to our Rosh Hashanah/Yom Kippur prayers is to be aware of the teaching in *Midrash Bereishis Rabbah* that "*Hakol b'kivui*, all good things require us to wait." To receive blessings, we must learn to wait for them.

Every day, morning and evening, from a month before Rosh Hashanah until the end of Succos, we end our *davening* with the same verse: "*Kavei el Hashem, chazak v'yaametz libecha, v'kavei el Hashem*, Wait for Hashem, strengthen and fortify your heart, and wait for Hashem". You prayed, you sent in your request? Now wait for an answer. Keep reminding yourself that Hashem has heard the prayer, and He wants to help, and your job is to wait and to wait some more, with an awareness that He is on His way.

The *Gemara* (*Shabbos* 31a) says that when after 120 years we arrive in Heaven, we will be asked: "*Tzipisa liyeshuah*, Did you await deliverance?" Since we are warned that we will be asked this question, it means that this is one of the skills we are expected to learn during our lifetime — the art of waiting.

Learning to wait for things is not a talent which comes naturally. Small children who want something want it RIGHT NOW, and part of growing up is to learn the meaning of the words "just a minute", or "later" or "not today." Even some grownups never learn this lesson completely, and it makes them very unhappy. They expect their first job to be perfect, and they expect their marriage to be problem-free from the start. When inevitable disappointments arrive, instead of taking them in stride and accenting the positive, they walk away; they just can't wait.

There's an apocryphal story about a yeshivah student who sought to become a *tzaddik*, and he went to an old, saintly rabbi for advice. "My son," the rabbi said, "if you wish to be holy, then, for the next 20 years, study Torah 16 hours a day. Eat and sleep the bare minimum, fast on Mondays and Thursdays, live in dire poverty and renounce all worldly pleasures. Do that for 20 years." The hopeful young man asked, "And after 20 years?" And the rabbi replied, "*Nu,* after 20 years you will be used to it!"

The goal of the Torah is not to live in poverty and pain. But learning to take difficulties in stride, to wait until the problems solve themselves, is part of becoming spiritually mature. And a special time to work on developing that maturity is Succos.

On Succos we sit in the *succah* to recall how Hashem cared for our ancestors in the Wilderness for 40 years. In the Wilderness each morning they awoke, and there was no food in the pantry, nothing at all. And each morning they waited, until Hashem made a daily miracle and *man* (manna) descended upon the camp. They waited daily, for 40 years.

We usually eat our Yom Tov meals as soon as we come home from *shul*, without delay — except the first two nights of Succos, if it rains. In that case, the mitzvah is to wait, not to eat immediately but to wait to see if the rain will stop. Surely the mitzvah is not to sit around grumpily complaining that Hashem did not make the weather to our satisfaction! The mitzvah is to wait and accept that either it will soon stop raining, or, if not, we will have the mitzvah of eating indoors. Either way, we train ourselves that life has its own schedule, and we must learn to adjust.

On Shemini Atzeres we begin saying, "*Mashiv haruach umorid hagashem*," a prayer for rain. But we do not actually begin to request rain until weeks later, when we say, "*v'sein tal umatar livrachah*." There is a timetable that cannot be rushed, just as our tradition tells us that in Heaven the Book of Life is written on Rosh Hashanah, sealed nine days later on Yom Kippur, and completely finalized during Succos on Hoshanah Rabbah. Everything has its time.

In the old days, people were better trained in waiting. The farmer could not hurry the planting season. He had to wait for rain, whenever it came. And what were the synagogues like in the days before clocks and watches? *Davening* did not begin at a precise hour. They *davened* "when it was time", more or less. You came to *shul* and you sat around, learning Torah or reading *Tehillim* or shmoozing with friends, and you waited. That was daily life.

Besides waiting for salvation, and prayers to be answered, this spiritual strength is vital to Torah study, to coping with tragedy, and to develop feelings of joy for mitzvos. In Torah, the Midrash says: "The fool says, there is so much to learn! I cannot learn it all," and he does nothing. But the wise man is patient and he learns two *halachos* today, and two more tomorrow, and little by little he achieves.

All people have their times of sorrow, times when they must cope with tragedy. But the *Gemara* says that seven things are hidden from human eyes, and one of the seven is *yom hanechamah*, the Day of Consolation, when Hashem will give the mourner strength to accept his sorrow and move on. Some people try to drown in self-pity, and others seek to forget their troubles. But the proper way is to allow yourself to feel the pain, and even to weep; but at the same time to know that there *is* a Day of Consolation, a day we have not seen but which we know will come. We feel the pain but we are not consumed by it, because the Day is coming, and we wait.

In taking on new mitzvos: A child goes off to sleepaway summer camp, and is terribly homesick. He waits a few days, feels better and enjoys the summer of a lifetime. If he does not wait, if his parents come to take him home right away, he misses out on it all. New mitzvos are often like that, very difficult at first. But if we know *Hakol b'kivui*, that for all good things one must wait, then we can stick to the mitzvah and wait it out, until the light of the mitzvah begins to shine.

Since this is the season we begin praying for rain, it's a good time to tell the true story of three Americans who purchased some land in Spain, potentially valuable property which they bought up cheaply because there was no water in the area. They believed they could find water by drilling for it, and then they would all be rich.

They drilled down 80 meters into the earth. No water. One of the three partners gave up, and he sold out to the other two at bargain prices. After another 20 meters of drilling, still no water. One of the two remaining partners sold his half share to the other, for next to nothing. The last remaining partner drilled down another 20 meters, and struck it rich.

Hashem does not give us everything we ask for, only those things that are good for us. But to acquire those things, we need to make the effort to ask, and then to wait, and wait some more. *Hakol b'kivui,* for all good things we must wait. But by waiting and not giving up, we can hope to be worthy of every blessing; and the awareness that we wait for our Father in Heaven is, in some ways, the greatest blessing of all.

FOUR SPECIES

On Pesach we remember how Hashem took us out from Egypt, and set us free. Shavuos recalls His gift of the holy Torah. And Succos is a reminder of Hashem's gift of physical nourishment, that He provides for our needs each and every day.

We celebrate Hashem's caring by sitting in the *succah*, symbolizing His protection which surrounds us, just as it surrounded our ancestors during their 40 years in the Wilderness. But on Succos we also have the mitzvah of shaking the *arba minim*, the four species of *lulav, esrog, hadassim* and *aravos*. What is the connection between Divine protection and a citron, a palm branch, myrtle leaves and willow twigs?

You probably know the classic explanation of *Chazal*, our Sages. *Esrogim* are edible, and they also have a pleasant aroma. *Lulavim* have no aroma, but they do bear fruit. *Hadassim* bear no fruit, but they are often pleasantly aromatic. *Aravos* have neither fruit nor aroma.

So too, the Sages said, there are four types of Jews. The *esrog* symbolizes Jews who possess both Torah learning and good deeds, fruit and aroma. The *lulav* is like those possessing learning but no special good deeds. *Hadassim* are Jews with good deeds but no learning. And *aravos* are Jews who have neither. On Succos we take all four species together as a sign of the essential unity in the Jewish people, "Let these come and atone for those."

Beautiful as the idea is, there are two problems, or questions, connected with it. Problem Number One: What does Jewish unity have to do with Succos? The theme of Succos is Divine protection, not unity. If you will argue that we must have unity as a prerequisite to be worthy of protection, then on Shavuos too, we must have unity to be worthy of receiving the Torah; but we don't shake a *lulav* on Shavuos.

A second problem, or question: From where did the Sages derive this explanation? Granted, it is perfectly understandable that the bringing together of different species is a symbol of some sort of unity, but is it so clear that these four forms of plant life are to symbolize these four types of Jews (Torah and good deeds, either/or, and neither)? Might it not just as easily be explained as a symbol of four personality types, like the four sons on Pesach? Or the four directions, or the essential unity of nature, the coming together of the entire cosmos?

It is entirely possible that our Sages' explanation is a tradition they possessed that went back to Mt. Sinai, and it is not something we could discover on our own. Even so, we always have a right to search for meaning, to try to comprehend why a particular explanation was given, if we can. So what do *lulav* and Jewish unity have to do with Succos, and how do we see that four species represent four types of Jews?

As noted above, Succos is a time to remember how Hashem cared for our people in the Wilderness, and how He continues to care for us today. It is therefore also a special time for us to count our blessings, and thank Hashem for life and health, friends and family and Torah and all good things, and to share these thoughts of gratitude with others. However, as the ethical classic *Chovos Halevavos* points out, a major obstacle to our appreciating good fortune is that every life also contains a certain amount of pain. Life's unavoidable sorrows are always ready to cast a shadow of unhappiness, and even if our days are 99 percent perfect, it is the remaining 1 percent that grabs our attention.

Along comes Succos to remind us that Hashem does care, truly. How much does He care? It is like a *succah*. *Succah* is a mitzvah that surrounds you, and even if you don't do anything, just being there makes you encompassed by the mitzvah. In the same way, Hashem's concern is total, fully encompassing each one of us. We may not always see it, just as if we sit in the *succah* with our eyes closed we will not see what surrounds us. But it's there.

The mitzvos of Succos begin at night, when we enter the *succah* to recall the Divine love and caring, the 99 percent of life which is joy. On the following morning, Hashem gives us the second mitzvah, *arba minim*, to take the four species to confront life's other 1 percent.

An *esrog* is a multipurpose creation. Hashem gave it taste and fragrance, and it can even be transformed into *esrog* jam or used in place of a lemon for a cup of tea, the sort of product we would expect from the Master Producer. Then we look at a *lulav*. Palm trees produce dates, but they have no special fragrance. Why didn't Hashem add an aroma, to make His creation perfect? Then we examine *hadassim*, fragrant, but with no food value at all; and *aravos* give us neither fragrance nor food. What a waste of Divine energy to create such things!

But our mitzvah is to take them all together, to proclaim that this negative outlook is in error. There is no waste in the Divine plan, and everything has its purpose. Just as we need all four species to fulfill the mitzvah, so too, the world needs all kinds of different people, animals, plants, natural phenomena and accidents of good fortune and otherwise. The way the world is arranged is the way which Hashem arranged, and, as the

Torah says, "Behold, it is very good."

In the famous Midrash, King David asked why Hashem created spiders. The Creator could have given him a scientific answer, but instead, when David was fleeing for his life and he hid in a cave, along came a spider to spin its web across the cave entrance. Enemy soldiers searching for David found the cave, but the unbroken spider web convinced them that David could not have entered the cave, and they left.

David thanked Hashem for answering his question; but he did not say, "Hashem, now I know why You made spiders, but what about grasshoppers?" He had learned his lesson that everything in the world has a purpose, and it takes time to discover what the purpose is. It may take years of study, or we may have to wait to learn the answers in *Olam Haba*, life after death; but whether or not we know them today, the answers are there.

As the *Alter* from Slabodka said: When the codes of *Rif* or *Rambam* omit *halachos* which we, based on our understanding of the *Gemara*, expected to find, then we know there is a reason for the omission and we expend much time and effort seeking to discover what the reason is. Then how much more so, when Hashem omits something from our own lives, anything which we, based on our limited understanding, expected to find; is it not clear that there must be a reason, and we must spend time and effort to discover what the reason might be?

You may recall the dismay in the 1980s when Yuri Andropov, director of the Soviet KGB, became head of the Soviet Union. With the KGB chief running the country, won't the situation for Soviet Jews, and world peace, become much worse? It was only with the passage of time that we realized that Hashem had put Andropov in charge in order to advance the career of Andropov's protegé, a man named Gorbachev. Once the plan was in motion, Hashem quickly removed Andropov from the scene, bring Gorbachev to power to enable him to cause the Soviet Empire to implode.

The anti-Gorbachev Soviet coup in 1991 made many people momentarily believe that advances in Soviet freedom had been canceled. Three days later Hashem showed us that the coup attempt was merely His way of bringing about the speedy death of communism, the coup de grace. The Creator always has a reason, and sometimes He allows us to see what it is.

(I ask the reader to please forgive the references to events which, to some readers, are ancient history. But so many events in the 1980s and 90s are such open *hashgachah pratis*, Divine Providence visible to all who look to see, and yet so many people fail to ponder their significance, that I thought them worth mentioning as examples of lessons that should not be forgotten.)

And therefore, we could suggest that when our Sages said that the four species symbolize four types of Jews, they meant it as an example of the broader principle that Hashem has a place for all types of diverse elements in His world plan, and four types of Jews are one of many examples illustrating the principle. *Lulav* and *esrog* must have *hadassim* and *aravos*, and in the same way, all of nature is planned to fit together, all human beings are interconnected, and certainly all Jews need one another to complete the plan. The lesson of Succos is that Hashem takes care, but the lesson includes viewing the world in its totality to comprehend what He is caring for, a larger perspective encompassing unity with all Israel, and with all the world.

Each one of us needs all of us. In a place of *tefillah* (prayer) or Torah learning, it is easy to see how each person adds to the atmosphere. But even other people, including those who make life difficult, have their purpose. Sometimes the purpose is to challenge us, or toughen us up, or to indirectly benefit us in ways we cannot perceive. But on Succos we take the four species, and we can fulfill this mitzvah in two different ways.

The simple way is merely to hold them. Picking up the four species is already a mitzvah (if done with intent to fulfill the Divine command), because just holding them together symbolizes that all the different parts of life have their place, they all fit in. But the more complete mitzvah is to wave the four species in every direction, like a signal flag. Waving is a public proclamation, signaling that the whole world should know Hashem's Creation has a plan, and all of it is needed; every Jew, every person, every atom, all of it is meant to be.

Shaking a *lulav* will not create instant *simchah*, especially to people focused on the 1 percent of sorrow, or to those individuals who are burdened with sorrows far beyond the norm. But the *lulav*, along with the *succah*, are annual reminders that the world is indeed a good place; it is Hashem's place, and each one of us has his place therein.

Perhaps this is why the Torah concludes its description of this mitzvah by telling us to take the four species *"usemachtem lifnei Hashem,* rejoice before Hashem." Because when we know that everything has its purpose, and that we too are part of the plan, that you and I truly belong here and are needed; that is what enables us to stand up with pride, knowing that all of us have the right and the honor to stand and rejoice, in the presence of Hashem.

REFLECTIONS ON AN ESROG

We know that the primary "meaning" of any *mitzvah* is that it is a Divine command, and the *mitzvah's* chief value for us is that it possesses the sanctity of fulfilling the Will of the Commander. However, we also know that most (possibly all) *mitzvos* are also meant to symbolize certain ideas, and to remind us of certain lessons. Sitting in the *succah* is the fulfillment of Hashem's command, but it is also a reminder of how Hashem cared for our ancestors in the Wilderness, for 40 years.

A single *mitzvah* can represent several ideas and numerous lessons, and *Rambam* (Maimonides) writes that we should study these lessons to the best of our ability. For now, let's examine a few ideas connected to just one part of a single Succos *mitzvah*, the *esrog*. The Gemara tells us that the *esrog* symbolizes the Jew who possesses both Torah learning and good deeds, so in selecting *mitzvos* to study an *esrog* is a good place to begin.

The Torah identifies the *esrog* as "*pri eitz hadar*, the fruit of the beautiful tree." But the Gemara (*Succah* 31b) adds that the word *hadar*, beautiful, also hints at another, similar word; the word *hador*, which means a dweller or resident. The Gemara explains that the Torah defines the *esrog* as the fruit which resides, which exists on a tree for more than a single season.

Most fruit trees produce a new crop each year, which grows and is harvested in the course of a few months. But an *esrog* can remain on the tree for several years, and on one tree there will be young and old *esrogim* at the same time, different generations of *esrogim* growing together. A great Chassidic teacher explained: The Torah goes out of its way to identify the *esrog* tree as multigenerational, to remind us that among Jews united by the Torah, there is no "generation gap."

Committed Jewish families have their troubles, especially living as we do surrounded by the influence of non-Jewish society. But in general, parents and children in Torah families have something to *share*. Most American teenagers have pictures of their heroes on their bedroom walls, pictures very different from those in the rooms of their parents. But in Torah homes, the photographs teenagers have of Torah Sages are the same as those honored by their parents. It is true that even Torah parents think their children's music is much too loud; but the words of the singers are words from the Torah, the same words the parents and grandparents sing.

There appears to be something in teenagers that makes them want to rebel. So in many Torah families, the boy decides one day to grow his *payos* long, and the girl demands longer skirts or *cholov Yisrael* cheese. Parents and children will never be the same; but the *esrog* reminds us that when we are all connected to the *eitz hachaim*, the same tree of life, all nourished by the same Torah and all growing at the same time, then we remain together, come what may.

Another well-known *esrog* characteristic is its distinctive shape. The halachah is that an *esrog* must rise to a point like a tower, and a spherical *esrog* is not valid. Perhaps this requirement (we find a similar one for the Kohen's turban in the *Beis HaMikdash*) is to remind us that Jewish life is about rising, growing.

If someone's life is spiritually stagnant, without any movement in Torah learning or *davening* or doing, then even if the person is virtuous, there is no real purpose for him to continue living longer; tomorrow will be no different from today. But someone rising, striving to make progress to climb to the top of the tower, then even if they never succeed, each day is full of meaning. That is an attitude with which to celebrate a Yom Tov.

Yet another well-known *esrog* characteristic is that if a branch of the *esrog* tree is grafted with a different fruit tree such as a lemon, the *esrog* is not kosher. *Esrogim* are rather delicate, and by grafting a lemon branch onto an *esrog* tree you can produce a much hardier fruit that looks just like a normal *esrog*. It will be identical in looks and taste and smell, it only differs in that it is not kosher; and shaking it on Succos is like shaking a banana, or one of those plastic lemons you can buy in the supermarket containing lemon juice.

The lesson is: It is very tempting to create Jewish ceremonies or experiences which *look* authentic, but are not. Conservative Judaism is notorious for preserving the outward *form* of a *mitzvah*, while tampering with its halachic *content* to the point of invalidation. At Pesach-time political groups have created their own so-called *seder*, so that there are "feminist *seders*" in which spilled wine represents women's suffering, "Peace Now *seders*" where divided matzah symbolizes the "*mitzvah*" to divide *Eretz Yisrael* into Jewish and Palestinian states, and even "Hebrew-Christian" *seders* where the four cups of wine are said to symbolize the blood of a dead Jew.

The great tragedy is that many an unsophisticated Jew sees the external forms (matzah, *maror*, wine) and thinks them Jewish, even when they are the very antithesis of Judaism. And these Jews may never come to move on to the real thing, because they believe that they already have it.

And therefore the fragile, expensive *esrog* comes to remind us: Yes, it would be easier and cheaper to adulterate the *esrog* with a lemon, and it would even look the same. But if you desire a true *mitzvah*, if you hope to tap into the spiritual power that will impact on your soul and the future of your children and grandchildren, then your only choice will be to use the real thing.

One more requirement for an *esrog* is that to be kosher, it must belong to you. After the first days of Succos, the *mitzvah* of *lulav* and *esrog* is performed only by decree of the Rabbis, and you may then use a borrowed *esrog* if you wish. But on the first day of Yom Tov (some say first two days) when the commandment is a Biblical obligation, then you must shake a *lulav* and *esrog* of your own.

One who has no *lulav* and *esrog* may use the loophole of accepting them from a friend as a gift, and then, after fulfilling the *mitzvah*, returning them as a gift to the original owner; but that is just a loophole if you are stuck. The Torah wants each Jew to *own* a *lulav* and *esrog*, not to borrow one. The symbolism is:

For all the previously noted lessons of the *esrog* — that generations should share ideals, that we must seek to climb the spiritual tower, and that we cannot dilute authenticity by grafting on other branches — and many more lessons, it is not enough to *borrow* them. We must acquire them, to make them our own.

Rav Yisroel Salanter *zt"l* used to say: "If only the great person would live up to the ideals of even the little person!" This means that there is a vast gulf between the way we know we should act and the way we actually do act, and even great Jews do not usually live up to the standards which are acknowledged in theory by the little ones. In theory we know the virtues — to be honest, kind, loving, hard working, humble, loyal, devoted to learning Torah and serious *davening,* and to give abundant *tzedakah* with a smile — is nonetheless, they are not quite *real* to us.

Another name for Succos in the Torah is "*Chag HaAsif,* the Festival of Ingathering." Commentators say that this is to hint to us that now is the time to gather in all our best thoughts; to reflect on our ideals to try to make of them something real, to feel the nourishing truth of at least one stalk of spiritual grain. And the requirement to own the *esrog* reminds us that our desire should be to make some spiritual acquisition truly ours, to make some ideal part of our daily thoughts to nourish us all through Succos, with an aftertaste to remain with us at least through Simchas Torah, if not beyond.

SUCCAH VS. LULAV

Since the Yom Tov of Succos is intended to remind us of how Hashem cared for our ancestors for 40 years in the Wilderness, the celebration would be appropriate in any month of the year. Commentators ask: Why does the Torah command that Succos is to be in the month of Tishrei?

Many possible explanations have been offered (the chapter "Cloud Cover" offers one). Here is one more: Other Yamim Tovim commemorate spiritual blessings like the Exodus, Revelation at Sinai and Atonement. But Succos is to remember the material blessings, thanking Hashem for sustaining us in the past and reminding ourselves that He continues to do so in the present. In *Eretz Yisrael*, Succos is the time people begin to look forward for the life-giving rains, and this is the time when we all say "*Mashiv haruach umorid hageshem*"; so this time was chosen to recall that it is Hashem Who has provided us with all our material needs since the beginning.

With this idea in mind, we can now explore another difference between Succos and other Yamim Tovim. Most Yamim Tovim give us one main *mitzvah* to perform, or a group of closely related *mitzvos*. Pesach has the *seder*, Rosh Hashanah the *shofar*, and Yom Kippur has the fast. But Succos seems to have two completely separate *mitzvos*, dwelling in the *succah*, and shaking the *lulav* and *esrog*. Why two?

The *mitzvah* to dwell in a *succah* is in effect every day of Succos, but the Torah's *mitzvah* is for us to take *lulav* and *esrog* only on the first day of Yom Tov. In the *Beis HaMikdash* (Holy Temple) it was a *mitzvah* to take the *lulav* every day, but elsewhere only on the first day. After the *Beis HaMikdash* was destroyed, the Rabbis instituted the taking of the *lulav* each day as a remembrance of the *Beis HaMikdash*, but that is only a Rabbinic decree, while *succah* is Biblical. Why did the Torah make a distinction between *succah* and *lulav*?

Perhaps the answer to both questions is: In using and enjoying material possessions and pleasures, all the good things we have and the activities which take up our time, we need to be guided by two general principles. The first is to know that it is Hashem Who cares for and protects us, and Who bestows on us all the goodness we enjoy. We must do our part to make a living and succeed, but in the end, success is only from him.

The second principle is to know that the purpose of all our possessions, and the aim of all our activities, should be to use what we have to serve Hashem as His representative on earth. Wealth is for *tzedakah* or other *mitzvos*, or to provide what we need to live worthwhile Jewish lives. Intelligence, physical strength and every talent should be directed towards spiritual goals, and our occupation and even time spent on recreation should all be geared to leading the life of a servant of Hashem.

The first principle, that Hashem is the provider and protector, is the message of the *succah*, reminding us how Hashem sustained us in the past and continues to do so today. The second principle, that all I have is to be directed to serving Hashem, is represented by the *lulav* and *esrog*. A *lulav* is a palm branch, perhaps symbolizing building materials and wealth. An *esrog* is food. *Hadassim* are fragrant, symbolizing emotional enjoyments like perfume, art, music and friendship. And *aravos*, insignificant branches, perhaps represent all the assorted trivia in our lives. I take them all together with a *berachah*, and wave them in every direction to proclaim: Wherever I turn, whatever I possess, is used to demonstrate my allegiance to Hashem.

But why is the *mitzvah* of *succah* every day, while the Torah commands *lulav* and *esrog* only once? Perhaps because the true *mitzvah* of *lulav* and *esrog* much more difficult to fulfill. *Succah*, to acknowledge Hashem as the source of all I possess, is possible for all of us, at least on an intellectual level if not in the depths of the heart. But *lulav* and *esrog*, to say that everything I have and do is devoted to Hashem, is at best an ideal, not a reality for most of us. One time, on the first day of Succos, the Torah demands it: Become inspired, feel the potential, and with *lulav* and *esrog* proclaim that holiness is the purpose of all you have! But if we proclaim *every* day that all our possessions are used for Hashem, there is the danger that we will end up only fooling ourselves.

I once tried to encourage a prominent Jewish physician to study Torah. He said to me: "When I spend time in my medical research, studying the wonders of Hashem's creation, isn't that also Torah? I'm learning Torah all day!" He had a point, but he was deluding himself. Like gangster Al Capone, who claimed he devoted his life to humanity, helping them obtain "the lighter pleasures of life," he too had a point. But even when some goodness results from involvement in material things, it does not always make such involvement a *mitzvah*, and Capone did not become a spiritual person.

It is surely possible to bite into a chocolate bar and think, "Blessings from Hashem!" It is possible to plan a trip to Hawaii in order to contemplate the glories of the Creator's world. You can even watch a baseball game thinking, "I am now relaxing for the purpose of putting me in a pleasant mood, in order to daven a better *Minchah*." It is *possible* to think that way;

but to say that *we* are working, eating and relaxing with that intent uppermost in mind is nonsense.

Succah, reaffirming the truth that Hashem provides, is every day of Yom Tov and Chol HaMoed. *Lulav* and *esrog*, dedicating all I have to Hashem's service, is only one day. One day is the best I can hope for — except in the *Beis HaMikdash*. The *Beis HaMikdash* was the dwelling place of the *Shechinah*, the literally tangible presence of Hashem. In the *Beis HaMikdash* you could indeed come to feel a desire to devote body and soul to a holy life; so in the *Beis HaMikdash* the *mitzvah* of *lulav* and *esrog* was also performed every day. (For ways to apply this *lulav* and *esrog* devotion at least to some small extent all through the year, see "Unintended Consequences" later in this section.)

We have no *Beis HaMikdash* today, but the Rabbis created a *zecher*, a remembrance. Remembrance means: We do not want to forget that there was a time and place where Jews *did* feel that closeness to Hashem; there was a time when many people saw all their possessions as Divine blessings and sought to use them all for Divine purposes. We may not have it today; but we are not ready to relinquish remembering and dreaming about it, we are not going to say that holiness is outdated and Hashem is just an anachronism to Whom Grandfather used to pray. We may not have all the right feelings, but we remember them, and continue to proclaim the ideal.

We find a similar *zecher* on Simchas Torah. Not everyone danced in the *Beis HaMikdash*, only "*chassidim v'anshei maaseh,*" the saintly and those known for good deeds; because how can I dance before Hashem, how can I dance with Torah if I do not show true love for Torah in my daily life? But Simchas Torah is also a *zecher*, a remembrance, to remind ourselves that the Torah *is* a source of life, and it is an ideal which all of us *do* want to come to love.

We now understand why Succos falls at this time of year; to remember Hashem helping in the past as we ask Him to help again with rain in the present. We understand why Succos has two distinct *mitzvah* symbols, one to proclaim that Hashem is the Provider, the other to proclaim our ideal of using all our blessings to serve Him. We understand why the original *mitzvah* of *lulav* and *esrog* was given for only one day, because it is self-delusion to say that we are always dedicating our lives to Him, except in the *Beis HaMikdash* where the *mitzvah* pertained all seven days. And we now know why the Rabbis made a *mitzvah* of *lulav* for seven days, to remind us what was, and to encourage us to dream of what might be again.

When you sit in the *succah*, or hold the *lulav*, it is a superb time to activate your imagination and to daydream. Imagine yourself eating lunch and thinking, "I am eating in order to enjoy the blessings of Hashem and to be healthy to serve Him." Picture yourself eating dessert for the purpose of fulfilling the *mitzvah* of *simchas Yom Tov*. Imagine that, whatever your occupation is, you work as an act of *chesed* (kindness), providing some product or service to the client or customer, and making a living in order to support a Jewish family and to give *tzedakah*.

The idea is not to fool yourself, but to dream. And if a Jew dreams long enough, it creates a certain power which, with Hashem's help, makes all the most important dreams come true.

HIDDEN MITZVOS

The Yom Tov of Succos stands out as *zman simchaseinu*, the time of our rejoicing, more than any other time. The Gemara does not say why Succos is more joyous than Pesach or Shavuos; but we do find this special joy connected with special Succos *mitzvah* observances performed in the *Beis HaMikdash* (Holy Temple) in Jerusalem.

One of these *mitzvah* observances is the taking of *lulav* and *esrog* in the *Beis HaMikdash*, fulfilling the commandment "*usemachtem lifnei Hashem*, rejoice before Hashem," i.e. in the *Beis HaMikdash*.

Another Succos *mitzvah* was *nisuch hamayim*, the pouring of water on the *Mizbei'ach* (Altar) as a libation, a symbolic offering to Hashem. Hashem has no need of offerings, and He certainly does not eat or drink, but the offering expresses our desire to thank Him for His blessings, a token of gratitude, even if we have nothing more to offer. The Gemara says that this *mitzvah* was fulfilled in such an atmosphere of sacred joy that it elevated some of those present to the level of prophecy. *Simchas Beis Hashoeivah*, the celebration of preparing water for the Altar, is a celebration we no longer observe, but which many Jews still remember through singing and dancing on one or more nights of Chol HaMoed.

Yet another special Succos observance in the *Beis HaMikdash* was *hakafos*, a daily march around the Altar with branches of willow called *aravos* or *hoshanos*. We no longer have an Altar, but we remember it with daily *hakafos* on Succos, especially with the seven circuits of the *bimah* on Hoshana Rabbah, and the main rejoicing on Simchas Torah is again expressed in seven *hakafos*.

These *mitzvos* of the offering of water and the march of the Hoshanos *aravos*, two unique aspects of Succos *simchah*, have something else in common. Neither one is mentioned in the Torah.

The laws of all *mitzvos*, all the commandments Hashem told Moshe Rabbeinu, are either written in the Five Books of the Torah, or they are included in *Torah she'b'al peh*, the Oral Tradition, laws and details of law which Hashem told Moshe orally, and which were not written down until centuries later. For example, Hashem told Moshe not to light a fire on Shabbos, and that was recorded in the Torah; Hashem also told Moshe not to write on Shabbos, but that was not recorded in the *Chumash* and was transmitted as part of the Oral Tradition. Both laws are Divine commands of equal status, but one was inscribed on parchment, and the other inscribed only in the memories of the Sages, up until the Gemara was transcribed 1500 years ago.

These Oral Traditions also fall into two categories. One is called *drashah*, a law in the Oral Tradition which is also hinted at in the written tradition, if you are learned enough to look. The Sages had a comprehensive system of how to analyze the text to discover the unwritten law hiding beneath the surface, and thousands of these *drashos* are recorded in the Gemara and Midrash.

The second type of Oral Tradition is *Halachah LeMoshe MiSinai*, halachah that is neither written in *Chumash* nor even hinted at in a *drashah*, but whose sole source is that Hashem told it to Moshe on Mt. Sinai. Therefore, all of Hashem's *mitzvos* are either written in the Torah, or they are Oral Traditions alluded to in the Torah as a *drashah*, or they are Oral Traditions which have no written sources at all.

We do not know why Hashem chose one particular *mitzvah* to be written rather than transmitted orally or vice versa. But in general, the Midrash says that Moshe Rabbeinu asked Hashem why He did not want it all written down, and Hashem replied that if everything is written, the gentiles will take the book and claim it belongs to them, their holy scripture. By writing down only part, even if others plagiarize, the unwritten secret part remains solely with Hashem's children, the people of Israel.

This seems to say that much of the Torah was unwritten in order to retain its unique closeness to the Jewish people. We can therefore suggest that the further away a *mitzvah* is from the written Torah, the more intrinsically Jewish it is; the more hidden the *mitzvah*, the more it reflects Hashem's private relationship with us.

If this is correct, then an Oral Tradition which is a *drashah* is more "ours" than a commandment written explicitly (as the Gemara puts it, "A law derived from a *drashah* is *chaviv*," especially dear). And therefore the *mitzvos* which are most intimately our own (or most "Jewish," if you will) are *mitzvos* which are not even hinted at in writing, *mitzvos* the non-Jews cannot touch; the *Halachah LeMoshe MiSinai* laws whose only source is that Hashem told Moshe on Sinai, and Moshe passed them down to us.

And if this is true, then it is not at all surprising that two *mitzvos* of special *simchah* on Succos, the offering of water and marching with *aravos*, are two *mitzvos* not written in the Torah and not even in a *drashah*. They are both *Halachah LeMoshe MiSinai*, given privately to Moshe, as a sign of the intimate relationship between those two *mitzvos* and ourselves.

What is so special about offering water and marching with willow branches? Why are they considered special *mitzvos* for

Israel, hidden from the gentiles? Perhaps the reason is: Non-Jews are permitted to bring offerings of animals to the *Beis HaMikdash*. They can relate to the idea of spending money and making a sacrifice for the Almighty. But on Succos, Hashem's special gift to us is that we bring an offering without spending money, an offering without sacrifice. In effect, Hashem says: "An offering? Draw some water, it's free. And while you are down at the river, pick some *aravos* ("*arvei nachal*, willows of the brook"), they also won't cost you anything. Because, when there's a gift of love, the price tag isn't important."

As we have previously noted, there is a famous teaching of our Sages that the *esrog* symbolizes a Jew who possesses both Torah learning and *mitzvos*, the *lulav* or *hadassim* symbolize Jews with learning *or mitzvos*, and *aravos* symbolize the Jew who has neither. On Succos, the special *mitzvah* was done with *aravos*, so that even the lowliest Jew can also relate to Hashem. Hashem cares, and He is waiting for us to show that we care in return.

Of course, a Jew who does a *mitzvah* only when it costs nothing is not demonstrating love. But we need to know that however little we may think we have to give, we all have a contribution to make, and by doing our part we help sanctify the world in a way that is uniquely our own.

Emerson wrote that "rings and jewels are not gifts, they are substitutes for gifts; the only true gift is a portion of thyself." A sincere thank-you, a compliment, a word of encouragement are little things which bespeak a relationship, which can be worth more than the most costly package.

Succos can be expensive, with the costs of meat, wine, a *succah*, *lulav* and *esrog*, a "*mi shebeirach*" and *Yizkor*. But Succos is also a time to ask ourselves what we can do to show Hashem loyalty without spending any money at all. I know one man who makes a point of picking up any rubbish he sees on the floor of his *shul*. Another is careful to avoid all conversation during *davening*, and another makes a point of coming to *shul* extra early. There are so many little things we can do that it pays to seek out a few more small gifts, even if only for the duration of the Yom Tov.

We may not be great *tzaddikim*. But even the lowly *aravah* gets a chance to walk around the *mizbei'ach*; and Succos is a time for us to add to our sense of self-respect by considering what inexpensive gift of the heart we have to offer.

I once received a handmade birthday gift from one of my daughters when she was 5 years old, an arts-and-crafts project which was totally useless to me. But to me it was precious, because the gift was her own idea. In the same way, we can all find some small gift to offer Hashem; a deed, a private *tefillah* (prayer), even a private thought, e.g., how many people think about Hashem on the subway? An inexpensive gift, but when Hashem sees it comes from His children, who offer it because we want to *be* His children, that makes it precious to Him; perhaps so precious that it will be a step towards His bringing the *simchah* of the *Beis HaMikdash* back again, if not this Succos, then the next.

WHO'S WORTHY?

Succos is *zman simchaseinu*, a special time for rejoicing. The Gemara (*Succah* 51a) tells us that in the *Beis HaMikdash* (Holy Temple) there was a celebration each night of Chol HaMoed Succos, all through the night. Music, singing and dancing was led by the greatest Torah sages. Giants of holiness would turn somersaults or juggle flaming torches, each one contributing whatever he could to the *simchah* of Yom Tov.

One of these merrymakers was the great Hillel. The Gemara tells us that Hillel would say, as he rejoiced: "*Im ani kahn, hakol kahn. Im eini kahn, mi kahn?* If I am here, everyone is here. If I am not here, no one is here."

At first glance this appears to be a display of vanity, Heaven forbid. "If I am not here, no one is here," as if he is the only significant person; like David Rockefeller, who never wore a wristwatch, because he knew, no matter how late he showed up, the meeting would not begin until he arrived. But that cannot be the meaning of this Gemara, because elsewhere the Gemara tells us that Hillel was famous as the most humble of men.

Some commentaries suggest that Hillel was talking as if he was speaking in the Name of Hashem, and his point was that meaningful *simchah* comes only from a relationship with Hashem and not mere drunken revelry. Hillel said, as if quoting the Creator: "If I, Hashem, am here, then everyone is here," i.e. there is reason for us to celebrate. "But if I, Hashem, am absent, if they celebrate without thinking of Hashem, then no one is here," the celebration is completely meaningless.

That interpretation will fit the words, but with difficulty. It is somewhat of a stretch to say that Hillel is speaking in the name of Hashem, when the Gemara does not mention it.

A different explanation was offered by the Frankfurter Rav, author of *Sefer Haflaah*, 250 years ago. Hillel's intent was to respond to the many sincere people who came to the *Beis HaMikdash*, and who wondered: "Is it truly possible for someone like me to be close to Hashem? I have my sins, I am not learned enough, and I do not even have a strong enough religious feeling. How can I expect to serve the Creator, and learn His Torah, and attempt to acquire true spirituality, and how can I pretend to rejoice with Him?"

To this Hillel replies: You are right. You are *not* worthy to be close to Hashem. But neither is anyone else. Hashem's greatness is so infinite that even the angels are unworthy. And yet, although we in no way deserve it, Hashem loves us, and calls us His children, and He desires every *mitzvah* we do, including this *mitzvah* to rejoice on Yom Tov with Him.

Hillel, the paragon of humility, would say: *Im ani kahn*, If I, who am not deserving of closeness to Hashem, can dance here, then everyone can dance. And on the other hand *im eini kahn*, if I cannot be here because I am unworthy, because in the scale of absolute values I am not holy enough, then *no* one can be here, because no one measures up, not even angels. And he danced, and encouraged others to do the same.

Teachers of *mussar*, Torah ethics and personal development, point out that almost everyone is burdened with a certain amount of arrogance, a vanity that makes us believe we are wiser or better or more deserving of honor than other people. At the same time, almost everyone suffers from a certain *lack* of self-esteem, an inner doubt of one's own intrinsic worth. These two apparent opposites are often related, as we see in cases of people who feel a need to boast or to degrade others in order to conceal the feelings of personal inferiority they feel within themselves.

One psychological theory is that we develop a lack of self-esteem in infancy, when the small child feels helpless and completely dependent on parental approval and affection. Whether or not this or any other theory is accurate, it seems likely that such feelings of insecurity which are so widespread are also rooted in the essence of the human condition, i.e. they also have a spiritual cause. Perhaps that root cause is:

Every human being, in his or her inner soul, knows that he or she stands before Hashem. And each of us is aware that, ultimately, we do not truly measure up. As the Gemara says, anxiety is connected to sin, the guilty knowledge that we are not who we should be.

And therefore Hillel said: Granted, you are not truly worthy; but no one else is either, not even angels. That is no excuse to keep on sinning, we must all do every *mitzvah* to the best of our ability. But our ultimate sense of self-worth, our right to stand in the House of Hashem, exists because Hashem wants us here, *He* says we are good enough. *Im ani kahn*, if I, Hillel, can be here, then so can every Jew. And if we measure with the yardstick of absolute perfection, then no one is here. And since Succos rejoicing is a *mitzvah*, then it means Hashem does consider us worthy, and all of us can come and rejoice.

We no longer have rejoicing in the *Beis HaMikdash*, but the *mitzvah* of *simchas Yom Tov* is still with us, and Succos is still a special time for these ideas, because on Succos we leave our homes for the *succah*. "A man's home is his castle," representing the material wealth in which we take so much foolish pride. Succos tells us to burst the bubble, to sit in a rickety hut and realize: Material possessions do not last. You cannot take them with you. And the value of your home does not define the value of your self. You exist only by the protection of Hashem, and just as He sheltered our ancestors in the Wilderness, so too is He the One Who shelters us every moment of every day.

"But if I cannot take pride in my possessions, if my self-worth is not defined by my bank balance, then what pride *can* I have?" The answer is: Pick up the *lulav*. The *lulav* is like a flag, a banner we carry to show that we are the standard-bearers of Hashem. We wave the *lulav* in all directions to demonstrate that *we* proclaim Hashem's control over the world, and *we* have the honor to strengthen the spiritual power wherever we go. In myself I am nothing, and I live in a broken-down *succah*. As the beloved child of Hashem I am everything, and I wave His banner with pride.

A popular politician used to speak to crowds of high school students, and he would tell them: "Repeat after me — 'I am SOMEBODY.'" But saying it does not make it so, and shouting does not still the voice of self-doubt within us. Instead, Succos tells us to face all our doubts, all our worries of whatever sort, and to say: "Yes, I have nothing! Only a rickety *succah*. But Hashem, the Master of the Universe, has everything! And He cares about me, and cares for me, and He has given me the mission to spread the sanctity of the *lulav* and every *mitzvah*, everywhere."

That knowledge gave Hillel the strength to dance in the *Beis HaMikdash*, and to call on others to join in; because all of us are within the circle of Divine love, and we all have reason to rejoice that Hashem has chosen us as His ambassadors, carrying His message of holiness and joy everywhere, every day of the year.

UNINTENDED CONSEQUENCES

Chapter 231 of the *Shulchan Aruch Orach Chaim* is entitled, "That All One's Intentions Should Be for the Sake of Heaven." Here is an excerpt: "...and in (sleeping) his intent should not be for physical pleasure, but to strengthen his body to serve Hashem *Yisbarach*. And so too in every way in which one enjoys this world, his intent should be only to serve the Creator, as it is written (*Proverbs* 3:6), 'In all your ways, know Him' ... and one who acts in this manner is serving his Creator constantly."

You may not normally view your coffee break as a holy act. But if you take the break in order to refresh yourself to be able to learn Torah, or to be able to *daven* better, or to be able to work harder in order to fulfill the *mitzvah* of supporting your family, then the coffee break itself is considered a *mitzvah*. There is a catch though, in that it appears you have to *mean* it, that your intent in eating and drinking truly *is* for the sake of the *mitzvah*; so for most of us who are not on that exalted a spiritual level, this chapter in *Shulchan Aruch* is not one we can fulfill.

Once every seven years, on the Succos which follows *Shemittah* (the Sabbatical year), the Torah commands that we come to Jerusalem to hear the king of Israel publicly read from the Torah to the nation; an affirmation that, in the famous formulation of Rav Saadiah Gaon, "Israel exists as a nation only by virtue of the Torah." Attendance at this gathering, called "*Hakhel,* assembly," is required for everyone: "*Hakhel es ha'am, ha'anashim v'hanashim v'hataf,* Assemble the nation, the men and the women and the little children" (*Deuteronomy* 31:12). And the Gemara asks: "Why do the little children come? In order to give reward to those who bring them" (*Chagigah* 3a, quoted by *Rashi*).

The Gemara's question is: Why does the Torah command us to bring children who are too young to understand anything that is being said? The Gemara's answer appears to be that, although there is no reason to bring little children, Hashem commanded it anyway, so that we would have yet another *mitzvah* for which to receive reward. But this explanation implies that the *mitzvah* is purposeless, a meaningless act which Hashem commanded merely to give us another *mitzvah*, which is difficult (if not outright blasphemous) to say.

But the *Sefer Yalkut HaUrim* explains as follows (I have seen this explanation quoted also in the name of the *Arizal*): On Succos, if each and every Jewish man and woman were required to attend *Hakhel*, what would parents of small children do for babysitters? There weren't any available, so one had no choice but to take the children along. Therefore Hashem said: Since you must bring the children anyway, let Me make it into a *mitzvah*, so that you should be rewarded for it.

This is a revolutionary idea. I am bringing my children only because I have no other place to leave them. But Hashem says, since this act is a necessary part of your *mitzvah* observance, I want to reward you for this too.

This principle holds true even today. Although your main intent is not for a *mitzvah* purpose, whatever is involved in your general Torah observance can have *mitzvah* value as well. However, *mitzvos tzerichos kavanah,* to obtain the *mitzvah* value you must think about it, to be aware you are involved in a *mitzvah*. But a little extra awareness is not so difficult, and a bit of thinking has spiritual power all by itself. For instance:

When a *tzaddik* brings a child to *shul*, the *tzaddik's* intent is for the child to be inspired by the *davening*. But if you are not such a *tzaddik*, and you brought your child to *shul* because it was the most convenient option, it is still part of your *shul*-going and therefore part of your *mitzvah*; and if you add the thought that in bringing the child to *shul* you *do* hope the child will pick up something good, your *mitzvah* value is all the greater. (Incidentally, *Tosfos Chagigah* 3a writes that people who bring small children to *shul* today do so based on the ancient practice of *Hakhel*! Of course, this applies only where the child will not disturb those who are *davening*.)

You sit down to your Shabbos or Yom Tov meal. You are eating not because of the *mitzvah*, but because you like to eat. Even so, Shabbos and Yom Tov meals are a *mitzvah*, and offer special elevation of soul, *if* when you eat you remind yourself that it is a *mitzvah*.

In fact, even if you are eating a weekday breakfast, and you are not the Chafetz Chaim who ate only to have strength to learn Torah and do *mitzvos*, nevertheless, without food you too will not be able to learn Torah or do *mitzvos*, and therefore your breakfast is also holy, *if* you take even the briefest moment to think about it.

The Chafetz Chaim once told a nonobservant Jewish pharmacist that he envies the pharmacist's *zechus*, the merit he has in Heaven for dispensing medicines; his *mitzvos* of *chesed*, daily acts of kindness, and sometimes even making the difference between life and death. The pharmacist objected that his motivation in dispensing medicine was not *chesed*, but to make a living. But the Chafetz Chaim replied: "Have in mind that in your work you are coming to fulfill the *mitzvos* of *chesed* and the saving of lives of people in the community; and even though you also make money for your livelihood, it does not detract from the value of the *mitzvah*, if your thoughts are for the sake of Heaven" (*Sefer LeShichno Sidreshenu*, Vol. II p. 31).

The pharmacist was not particularly devout, and the Chafetz Chaim surely did not expect him to suddenly push aside his self-interest and practice his profession mainly out of *chesed*. But he was advising him to *add* the goal of *chesed*, and this is something all of us can do. Whatever your job and whatever your primary motivation for working may be, the fact remains that your income does support your family, and it does enable you to give *tzedakah* and buy food for Shabbos and various other good deeds. As to the job itself, as long as it's not detrimental you are probably providing a service or product that gives other people something they need, or that adds to their happiness and well-being. Whatever the reason you work, add the *mitzvah* thought, and receive the benefit at no extra cost.

We do not have the *Hakhel* assembly today. But for a perfect illustration of how an everyday act can be transformed into something sacred, enter the *succah*. The *mitzvah* of *succah* is to do the most mundane, *nonmitzvah* activities — eating, shmoozing, snoozing — but by doing them inside the *succah* they become transformed into acts of *kedushah*, holiness. To sit with my friends and gab about national politics, over a bowl of potato chips or pretzels and a six-pack, fulfills a *mitzvah*? If I am sitting in the *succah*, it does.

There is holiness in human beings, especially in the children of Avraham *Avinu*. All we need is the right structure to bring it out, whether it is the physical structure of the *succah*, or the mental structure of being aware of the *mitzvah* value in daily activities. It is not that we should fool ourselves to think that our every trivial pursuit is a *mitzvah*, nor to fool ourselves to think that our primary motivation is altruistic even in the worthwhile things we do. But to recognize the *mitzvah* component where it exists, and to add the awareness that many of our activities help us come closer to Hashem, that perception has power in it; the power to add meaning to most everything we do, in our own eyes and in the eyes of Hashem.

A QUIET LOVE

Many people think of Shemini Atzeres as nothing more than the tail end of Succos, but the Gemara (*Rosh Hashanah* 4b) calls Shemini Atzeres "*regel bifnei atzmo*," a Yom Tov unto itself. The *korbanos* (sacrificial offerings) brought on Shemini Atzeres are very different from those offered on Succos, we do not shake *lulav* and *esrog*, and in *Eretz Yisrael* one may not even sit in a *succah* on that day.

Shemini Atzeres stands out from all the Yamim Tovim in two ways. The first is that there is no distinct *mitzvah* symbol associated with it. Rosh Hashanah has the *shofar*, Yom Kippur the fast, Succos has *lulav* and *succah*, Pesach has *matzah*, even Shavuos has the study of Torah; but Shemini Atzeres is "just a Yom Tov," with no individual *mitzvah*.

Shemini Atzeres' second distinction — one which most people have never considered — is that it is the only Yom Tov which does not commemorate any generally known historical event. Pesach recalls the Exodus from Egypt; Shavuos, the

Divine Revelation; Succos, the 40 years in the Wilderness; Rosh Hashanah, the creation of the world; and Yom Kippur, the day of the giving of the second Tablets at Mt. Sinai. But, as far as is generally known, Shemini Atzeres commemorates nothing at all.

If it is only this one Yom Tov that contains no ritual symbols, and no historical memories, and no hint in the Torah of any reason for it, that absence of meaning in itself makes Shemini Atzeres stand out by its very obscurity. The silence is so loud that the Yom Tov calls unusual attention to itself by saying nothing. To take an analogy from the Gemara (*Berachos* 58a), a royal parade went through town, and everyone cheered and shouted for each group of nobles who passed; but then suddenly all were silent, because the king himself had arrived.

In the annual cycle of Yamim Tovim, Pesach is reckoned first, then Shavuos, Rosh Hashanah, Yom Kippur, Succos, and finally the Yom Tov to which all others lead, Shemini Atzeres. There is a famous Midrash comparing Shemini Atzeres to a private dinner with the King; but since dining with kings are perforce foreign to most of us, let me take the liberty of updating the Rabbis' parable with a more contemporary one.

Picture a 22-year-old yeshivah student, who decides that the time has come to seek a wife. In traditional yeshivah circles dating is only for purposes of marriage, and the initial encounters are arranged by intermediaries, a friend or a *shadchan*. Generally, the parents make careful inquiries as to background and suitability. If they feel that the prospects are good, they will give their go-ahead for the next step. Our yeshivah student is informed about the young lady who appears to be what he is looking for, and she likes what she hears about him, so they arrange a first date.

He picks her up at her home, introduces himself (I'm told that some people consider this last step unnecessary, which I think is an error), and off they go for two or three hours of company and conversation. But before he does all this, he spends hours (if he is a novice) agonizing: What on earth are they going to talk about? Shall he spend three hours explaining to her his latest Gemara studies, or the intricate differences between different styles of Borsalino hats?

To solve this problem, he takes her to some place of light entertainment like a museum or a zoo, which provide opportunities to discuss the artworks or the elephants (tip: Do *not* compare the young lady to any of the ladies in the paintings or to any of the zoo animals, even if a compliment is intended). If the meeting goes well, they decide to meet again, going on to a succession of museums, restaurants, the aquarium, the aviary, and so on until both feel confident enough that they have found their life partner, and they decide to marry.

The next three months they are busy planning their wedding. Then there are two or three postnuptial months of setting up house and visiting all the relatives. Finally, when all the hassle is over, they sit down to a quiet supper together, just the two of them with no distractions; and *then* they discover, they have nothing at all to say to each other. This may be a problem — albeit a problem that is solvable.

Icebreakers to help open conversations are useful, and pleasant diversions shared can help cement a relationship. But if in the end, without these external aids you have nothing to say, if you cannot just sit and enjoy each other's company, then you don't have a relationship, only a theater companion. There must be at least some time when you can face the other person and tell yourself: I like being with this person, just because this *is* the person he or she is.

Another word in the Torah for Yamim Tovim is *moadim*, a word which literally means "meeting," a get-together (similar to the word *vaad*, a council). *Moadim* are times when we meet with Hashem, ideally in the *Beis HaMikdash*, but if not, then wherever we may be.

At the meetings, all the *moadim* (annual reunions, in a sense), we talk over all that happened in the good old days, and we also have concrete ceremonies to commemorate them. We have a Pesach *seder* and we relate the story of the Exodus from Egypt. We sound the *shofar* and say, "*Hayom haras olam,* today is the birthday of the world." We sit in the *succah* and recall the 40 years' journey under Divine protection. Finally, after the entire cycle of Yamim Tovim is concluded, Hashem says: "We've had a great year together, done so many things, relived so much of the past. Now come, let's have one day when we don't do anything special, and we don't have to commemorate anything in the past. Let's have a day when we are just together."

That last holiday, the true test of the relationship, is Shemini Atzeres.

And therefore Shemini Atzeres, which does not commemorate an event and which has no special *mitzvah* to perform, is in a special way a day to pause, to relax, and in place of doing, to savor the joy of just being. It is very pleasant to be alive; to eat, to walk, to enjoy the sunlight and the company of other people, and to recognize how all this pleasure is a gift of love from Hashem. On weekdays we are too busy with our work, and even on Shabbos and Yom Tov we can be too busy even with *mitzvos* to fully relax. Shemini Atzeres tells us "*Atzor,*" Stop! That's the meaning of the word *atzeres* — to stop and enjoy, to the fullest, the relationship you are so fortunate to enjoy.

Succos is also a harvest festival, a time when the farmer surveys all the crops brought in over the summer, and gives thanks to Hashem. Shemini Atzeres, the day after Succos, we begin to say, "*Mashiv haruach umorid hagashem,*" a prayer requesting rain for the harvest to come.

Sitting back and appreciating what we already have, and realizing Who it was Who gave it to us, is the best preparation to be able to ask for more and more in blessings both spiritual and material, looking forward to abundance for ourselves and for all who share the blessings of Hashem's special love.

KOHELES AND SUCCOS

I t is a centuries-old custom to read the Book of *Koheles* (*Ecclesiastes*) sometime during Succos, most often on Shabbos Chol HaMoed. As with a number of other *minhagim* which postdate or are not mentioned in the Gemara, the exact reason for this custom is no longer known with certainty. Commentators can only speculate, and the most well-known hypothesis is that since Succos is a special time of rejoicing, the rabbis were afraid we might get carried away and do something wrong. They therefore instituted the reading of *Koheles*, with its somber pessisism, in order to keep us sober.

Let me suggest an additional reason for *Koheles*. At the close of Yom Kippur, we sound the *shofar* as a sign that the Jewish people have been forgiven. The Midrash says that at that moment, a voice rings out in Heaven to proclaim: "Go, and eat your bread in happiness, and drink your wine with a glad heart, for Hashem is pleased with your deeds."

That Heavenly announcement is a quotation, a verse from the Book of *Koheles* (*Ecclesiastes* 9:7); and perhaps it is for this reason that we read *Koheles*, to demonstrate that the Succos eating and drinking are an expression of thanks to Hashem, for His forgiveness on the Yom Kippur just completed.

The next verse (9:8) states: "*Bechol eis yihiyu vegadecha levanim*, At all times let your clothes be white." Clothes worn while doing manual labor are not white, because they get soiled too easily (hence the expression "blue-collar worker"). White was reserved for festival days, and *Koheles* states, metaphorically: Let your clothes always be white, live in a state of celebration, joy at all times. He is not coming to tell us to quit our jobs, but to teach that this is the proper emotional state for a Jew; continuous, total joy.

However, along comes the Gemara to turn this verse on its head. The Gemara in Shabbos says, "At all times let your clothes be white" means at all times be prepared for the day of death. Mentally, walk around wearing your white shroud, always. This is a call to repent. The Gemara in *Berachos* says that one who is fighting a losing battle against temptation to do evil should remind himself of the day of death — instant shock therapy.

Such frightening thoughts certainly have their place, in the proper measure and the proper time, although it is striking that this Gemara (or the verse in *Koheles* itself) says that we should think these thoughts "at *all* times." But what is most unusual about the Gemara is that it is giving us an interpretation which is the exact opposite of the plain meaning of the verse! It is common for the Sages in the Gemara, and even more so in the Midrash, to give an explanation which adds a deeper understanding to *complement* the plain sense of the verse. But here, *Koheles*' command to rejoice is taken as an invitation to a funeral, the white wedding dress changed to a shroud. Why did the Sages do this?

The simplest answer is that the Gemara is doing what it always does, providing an insight into the plain meaning of the verse. *Koheles says*, Rejoice! But how? What gives continuous joy? The Gemara explains that it is not the eating and drinking, not the pleasure of life. Instead, the great joy is when you are able to appreciate how precious life itself is.

A friend of mine is the spiritual leader of a prominent congregation in the Midwest. One year, the morning of *Shabbos Shuvah* (the Shabbos between Rosh Hashanah and Yom Kippur, when the Rabbi traditionally delivers a major *drashah* or lecture), my friend suffered a sudden attack of severe pain, from unknown causes. Instead of *shul*, he spent *Shabbos Shuvah* in the hospital. *Baruch Hashem*, everything turned out well, and he is now in excellent health.

When I heard the news the next day, I called him at the hospital and said: "Reb Zev, I am so happy for you! Being the Rav of a *shul* myself, all year I constantly worry, 'What will I say in my *Shabbos Shuvah drashah*? When will I find time to prepare my talk?' But you, because you took ill the day you were to deliver your *Shabbos Shuvah drashah*, your prepared talk is still in your word processor. For the next 12 months you can rest easy, knowing you are set! What greater joy can a rabbi have?"

However, happy as I was for him, he explained to me that he was much happier. Why? Because, he said, yesterday he was rushed to the hospital emergency room, not knowing what would happen, and today he sees, he's alive!

Speak to a hospital patient who has successfully undergone organ transplant surgery. Speak to the parents of a child who has successfully undergone any sort of surgery. That is where you see true *simchas hachaim*, the joy of life itself. And the Gemara is explaining that this joy, *Koheles'* white garment of celebration, is available to all of us. All we need to do is to imagine ourselves in those other white garments, all the time, meaning: to live this day, as if it was our last.

Rabbi Eliezer ben Hyrkanos used to say (*Avos* 3:15), "Repent one day before your death." His disciples asked, How can one know which day that will be? He replied: Then repent every day, for perhaps this one will be the last. Rav Yitzchak Isaac Sher *zt"l* (Slabodka Rosh Yeshivah, quoted by Rav

Yechiel Yaakov Weinberg of Montreaux *zt"l*) taught that Rabbi Eliezer is not encouraging us to go into mourning. Instead, he is affirming the enormous importance of being alive, that we should not sleep through our days, but learn to value each day we are granted.

My wife and I are blessed with a married daughter who lives in *Eretz Yisrael*. Every so often she phones, and I get to hear her voice. I love every minute of it, and, at the price of long distance, the minutes are all too few. And after we hang up, I look at my other children, the ones I sometimes take for granted; and I enjoy *their* voices all the more.

Is it not strange that on Yom Tov, a time of celebration, we say the memorial prayer of *Yizkor*? Why think of departed loved ones, why open old wounds, on a day of joy? These are people we dearly miss, for whom we would give so much to be able to see again — and *that* is a reason why *Yizkor* is said on Yom Tov, because *Yizkor* reminds us how precious love is; how precious all our living relatives, friends, neighbors and all those Jews sitting together with us in *shul* are.

What would I say to my family if today's conversation was one of farewell, if today was my last one? What kind of *Shemoneh Esrei* would I *daven*, if I knew that I would never be able to *daven* again? During the Holocaust, when Jews spent their last Shabbos in *shul* before the deportations, did they interrupt their prayers for small talk, or did they hold the *siddur* in passionate embrace? "At all times let your clothes be white," as if these few hours were all you had left, that is the key to joy.

The traditional Yom Tov greeting is "Good Yom Tov!" (or "Gut yontiff," which means the same thing). An old *shammos* pointed out to me that this appears to be a redundancy, because the word "Yom Tov" itself means "a good day." Why wish one another a "Good good-day"?

Perhaps the meaning is: Whoever we are, whatever our life is like, we Jews know: This day is good. We know it is good because, however difficult our personal situation may be, at the onset of Yom Tov every Jew has the *mitzvah* to recite the *berachah* of *Shehechiyanu*, "Thank You, Hashem ... for keeping us alive and for sustaining us, and for bringing us to this day." And we know the day is good because Hashem commands us to set aside almost the entire Torah in order to save a Jewish life, without regard to the "quality" of that life. It is all worthwhile, to be able to live one more day, because the day is truly good.

And so we bless one another — every greeting is a blessing, a form of prayer ("Good morning" = May Hashem bless you with a good morning, etc.) — and we say "Good Yom Tov." "Good Yom Tov," "Good good-day," means: This day of goodness, may Hashem help you to feel it, and to draw the goodness out, in *mitzvos*, in relationships, and in just being alive. "*B'yom tovah heyei b'tov*, On a good day, have goodness" (*Ecclesiastes* 7:14, of course). And "go, and eat your bread in happiness, and drink your wine with a glad heart, for Hashem is pleased with your deeds."

If we wear the white clothes, with the proper perspective, that will give us the "glad heart" for drinking, eating, and acting in a way that Hashem will be pleased with our deeds. And then we will truly be able to wish each other a good Yom Tov, drawing out all the goodness; with hearts that even at *Yizkor* experience the joys, both luscious and bittersweet, of hearing the voice that rings out in Heaven to remind us how precious every day is.

WHY CHANUKAH?

Each Yom Tov in our calendar has its own special *mitzvos*, and each Yom Tov also has its own special message to ponder and to share with our families. If we light candles or eat matzah or sit in a *succah* without reflecting on the meaning of the *mitzvah*, the Yom Tov is incomplete, a body and heart without the complement of the mind.

As we have previously noted, on Pesach we remember how Hashem rescued us, and set us free. Shavuos recalls His giving us the Torah; Succos, that He provided for our material needs; Rosh Hashanah, that He judges; Yom Kippur, that he forgives. But what is the special meaning of Chanukah?

If Chanukah is a reminder that Hashem saved us and gave us independence, we have already seen that lesson in the eight days of Pesach. If Chanukah is intended to teach that He performs miracles for us, Pesach teaches the same lesson with many more miracles, and miracles far more spectacular than the oil burning in the *Menorah* for eight days. What is the unique contribution of this holiday, which necessitated its inclusion in the Jewish calendar?

In the prayer of *Al HaNissim*, (added on Chanukah to the *Shemoneh Esrei* and *Bircas HaMazon*), we give thanks for our salvation with these words: *"Masarta giborim b'yad chalashim, v'rabbim b'yad m'atim, u'temei'im b'yad tehorim, u'resha'im b'yad tzaddikim, v'zeidim b'yad oskei sorasecha.* Hashem, You delivered the strong into the hands of the weak, the many into the hands of the few, the impure into the hands of the pure, the wicked into the hands of the righteous, and the wanton into the hands of the diligent students of Your Torah."

All that is certainly true. But it is radically different from the prayers we offer on every other Yom Tov.

On Pesach, we thank Hashem profusely, but we hardly mention Moshe Rabbeinu. We focus solely on the Creator and we give Him all the credit; there was no human intervention. On Chanukah, although we give great thanks to Hashem, we also stress the role of human beings — the victory of the few, the pure, the righteous students of Torah — and this makes the message of Chanukah unique.

Chanukah has its place in the calendar to teach us something beyond the lesson of Pesach, and that lesson is: Pesach demonstrates that Hashem possesses infinite power, and that He desires to use that power to help us. But Chanukah demonstrates that Hashem also desires to use that power to *help us help ourselves.*

At the first Pesach, the Jewish people were passive, while Hashem waged war against Egypt on our behalf. But at the first Chanukah, it was the *Chashmonaim*, the Maccabees, who themselves waged war. The *Chashmonaim* did not have an army that could stand up to the Syrian-Greek phalanx. They were few, and they were weak. But *masarta*, Hashem delivered their enemies *into their hand*; not just a rescue, but Hashem gave them the power whereby they would win a victory on their own.

We do not see many open miracles today, and we often find ourselves alone, facing formidable obstacles in our personal lives, and in our collective life as a Jewish community. But even without open miracles, if we *daven* sincerely, and if we dedicate ourselves to aspiring to live up to Torah ideals, then we can sense that Hashem is still with us, and still all-powerful; and He stands ready to use His power to assist us — all of us — to help us find our own ways through difficult situations, and to win.

A destitute widow came to the prophet Elisha to beg for help (*II Kings* 4:1). He replied: "What can I do for you? Tell me, what do you gave in your home?" She had nothing, except for one jar of oil. But Hashem gave Elisha the power to perform a miracle, and the single jar kept pouring without stop, until it filled a warehouse-full of barrels. Commentators point out that with all of Elisha's power, even he could not make something out of nothing. Even for a miracle to occur, it was necessary for the beneficiary herself to provide some small thing with which to begin, at least one jar of oil. Once *we* make a beginning, Hashem will help us to persevere through to the end.

Elisha's jar of oil was a portent of the oil of Chanukah. A small jar of oil burned in the *Menorah* for eight days, a miracle; but the miracle occurred only after the Jews had lit the *Menorah* with oil for one day, using all the oil they had. The military victory over the Syrian-Greeks was also a miracle; but it was achieved only after a handful of people with courage went out to battle, waging war with all the limited resources they possessed.

Since those days, the Creator of the Universe has not gone into retirement. In mid-19th-century Germany, traditional Judaism was dying, and it was widely believed that no modern person would remain loyal to the Torah. But in 1851, 11 families in Frankfurt-am-Main started a private Orthodox *minyan*, and Rabbi Samson Raphael Hirsch became their spiritual leader. Within 40 years the congregation had grown to include 500 families, Europe's first Orthodox day school, and a comprehensive ideology of facing the world's challenges which guided Jews in Germany, and many thousands more even to this day.

Similarly in the United States, the American Torah resurgence is a 20th-century miracle. But that miracle was possible

only because of the handful of modern Maccabees who refused to surrender, and who organized synagogues and day
schools and yeshivos and Torah-loyal organizations across the
country. Hashem's help multiplies the power of a single individual by a hundred or a thousand times; but like the zeros
after a number, the effect is only if there exists a number with
which to begin.

Two tiny islands lie off the coast of Japan, each of which is
no bigger than a king-size bed. Nothing grows on them, and
they have no intrinsic commercial value at all. Nevertheless,
the Japanese government has spent *several hundred million
dollars* to keep these islands from crumbling into the sea. The
reason they do this is that, under international law, as long as
this minuscule piece of real estate remains above water, the
surrounding ocean is considered Japanese territorial waters;
and Japan retains all fishing rights and other territorial advantages for many hundreds of square miles.

It is an apt metaphor. One person alone can do little. But
one person keeping his head above water, one person refus-
ing to surrender to the waves that wash over us, can bring
down Divine blessings and aid, to make an impact far beyond
his own time and place and innate ability.

It is no coincidence that Hashem arranged for the miracle
of Chanukah to occur at the beginning of winter. Every human being goes through periods of darkness and cold, and our
people as a whole often find themselves facing an uncertain
future, trapped in a tunnel with no visible light at its end. But
Chanukah teaches us that if we will only persevere, no matter the adversity, to do what we can to fight the good fight,
and to light what small jar of oil we possess, then the day will
come when Hashem will give us victory, and we will all be able
to celebrate, with Hallel and *latkes*, and songs of joy.

HILLEL AND SHAMMAI

The Gemara (*Shabbos* 21b) records a well-known difference of opinion between the schools of Hillel and Shammai concerning the preferred way to kindle the Chanukah lights. Beis Hillel say to light one candle the first night of Chanukah, two candles the second night and three the third, and so on to eight candles on the eighth and last night. But Beis Shammai say to light eight candles the first night, seven the second night, and continually decrease the number by one until, on the last night of Chanukah, only a single candle is lit.

Of course, today we follow the opinion of Beis Hillel; but Beis Shammai's view is difficult even to understand. Although Beis Shammai found parallels to their approach in the Torah, it seems so anticlimactic to decrease the number of lights as the holiday goes on, as if the later days were not as important. What was Beis Shammai's ultimate reason, and what is the fundamental point on which Beis Hillel and Beis Shammai disagree?

Rav Shlomo Yosef Zevin *zt"l* offered the following explanation: A candle (or oil lamp) is a fire, a burning flame. It is also light, a source of illumination.

In the *mitzvah* to light a fire on the *Mizbei'ach*, the Sanctuary Altar, the chief purpose of that fire was not to illuminate but to burn, to consume the sacrifices. As the Torah says, *eish tukad*, a burning fire on the *Mizbei'ach* (*Leviticus* 6:6). With regard to other *mitzvos*, like Shabbos candles, the main purpose is not to burn but to illuminate. This is why, if Shabbos candles are unavailable, many authorities permit the use of electric lights instead (Rav Yosef Henkin *zt"l* and others), because the light is more important than the burning flame.

For Chanukah, we require both aspects, both light and a flame. This is a reason why electric menorahs may not be used on Chanukah, and why the candles must be placed where they are visible. We need a true flame, from a candle or oil lamp, and we also need to see (though not use) its illuminating light.

Rav Zevin explained: The idea of "light" is used in the Torah to symbolize spirituality, and the Torah itself. "*Ki neir mitzvah v'Torah ohr*, For a mitzvah is a lamp, and Torah is the light" (*Proverbs* 6:23), and "*Neir Hashem nishmas adam, chofeish kal chadrei baten*, A man's soul is the lamp of Hashem, illuminating the inner recesses of the heart" (*Proverbs* 20:27). Light represents the power of the Torah, and the power of goodness to light up the dark places in the soul, and in the world.

Fire, however, the burning flame, is used to symbolize the destruction of evil, all that is harmful in the world. In punishing the wicked, the Torah commands: "*uviarta hara mikirbecha*, you shall burn up the evil from your midst" (*Deuteronomy*, 13:6, 17:7, 19:19, 22:21, 22:24, 24:7). In the Rosh Hashanah *Shemoneh Esrei* we pray that "*harish'ah k'ashan tichleh*, may wickedness by destroyed like smoke," that all forms of evil be eradicated from the world and from ourselves.

Chanukah candles are a burning flame, symbolizing the destruction of the negative, the burning up of all that is bad. The candles are also a a light, symbolizing the triumph of the positive, the light of Torah and all that is good.

These two elements, removing the negative and building up the positive, were two aspects of the original Chanukah story. The Maccabees had to battle against the oppression of the Syrian-Greeks, and also against the influence of Greek paganism and hedonistic materialism, to vanquish it and to burn it up. But Chanukah also meant the rededication of the *Beis HaMikdash* (Holy Temple), and rededication to the positive aspects of Judaism in general. We say in the *Al HaNissim* prayer that the Maccabees were *oskei sorasecha*, they were diligent students of Torah, because they saw that the spiritual light had to spread for Israel to survive.

Our *mitzvah* of Chanukah lights today is to commemorate the burning flame, to destroy the bad, and also to recall the light of Torah and the *Beis HaMikdash*, to spread the good. But which aspect is more important? Although we need both, which aspect is more necessary for us to focus on, as individuals and as a nation?

To this question Beis Shammai answers: Before you can develop the positive, you must first uproot that which is negative. Someone who approaches the Torah with non-Jewish attitudes will end up interpreting the Torah in a false, non-Jewish manner. Someone who is not pure of heart, who is not pure of character, is not yet ready to enter the world of spiritual ideals.

Beis Hillel will agree that Beis Shammai has a valid point. But if you cannot begin the quest for the good until you have purified yourself from all that is bad, you may never come to know what goodness truly is. If a person places his entire focus on his faults, if a person has low self-esteem and thinks himself unworthy of anything holy, his negative self-evaluation may be accurate; but the only way to overcome that is to accentuate the positive, to enter the world of Torah and allow the Torah's light to spread its illuminating effect.

Almost 30 years ago, in a Brooklyn yeshivah high school, there was a teenager who was blessed with a good mind and a diligent nature, but who had very little interest in the Torah. Torah learning was not for him; he had grown a hippie-style beard, and as his high school graduation approached there was a concern that he might abandon *mitzvah* observance entirely.

Had I been his teacher, I would have tried to persuade him to take a few months after graduation to attend a summer Torah program in *Eretz Yisrael*, to at least give him some exposure to post-high school Torah learning. But his 12th-grade Rebbi was an astute man, who told him: A young man with your abilities should spend the summer learning in the yeshivah of Lakewood, New Jersey.

The Lakewood yeshivah student body consisted of older, serious students. It was not geared for a boy graduating high school with a hippie's beard, but the boy was awed by his Rebbi's compliment. He applied to Beth Medrash Govoha in Lakewood, the Rebbi pulled some strings to get him in, and when the boy encountered the full power of Torah, it lit up his life. In three months the hippie beard became a "*yeshivishe*" beard, and today this man is a respected *talmid chacham* (Torah scholar).

Sometimes, the best defense is a good offense. And sometimes, the best way to fight the negative is to discover the positive in your life, as it exists today.

The contrasts between Shammai and Hillel can be illustrated by the famous story of the non-Jew who came to Shammai with the intention of converting to Judaism, but with the stipulation that the Jews would appoint him *Kohen Gadol*, High Priest. Shammai saw that the gentile was approaching the Torah without having rid himself of negative traits of character, ego and status-seeking, and Shammai threw him out. But Hillel took him in and learned Torah with him, until the man saw, through the light of Torah, what true glory is, and his foolish status-seeking fell by the wayside on its own.

Beis Shammai say: The first lesson of Chanukah must be to rid of ourselves of the bad, to burn it up. We therefore kindle eight lights the first night and one fewer each successive night, to show that the bad is becoming less and less. But Beis

Hillel say: The more vital lesson is the *light* of Chanukah, the rededication to holiness and the illumination of Torah. With Torah light, the more we learn, the more light we produce; so we therefore increase the number of each night's candles, to show the growth of the positive.

Beis Shammai and Beis Hillel are two aspects of a unified truth. We cannot ignore the negative, and we must confront the self-destructive behavior patterns of laziness, envy, arrogance and rationalization that do so much harm. But sometimes, the best way to begin is to accent the positive, to find a *mitzvah* or an area of Torah study that appeals to us, and work at it; to try to develop a positive self-image and a positive relationship with the Torah, and to discover a way to connect with the light of Torah, to feel it illuminate our lives.

Too many people mistakenly think that the fullness of Torah is only for rabbis, or *tzaddikim*, or Jews who are by nature more "*frum*" than the person doing the thinking. But it is not true. The whole Torah is for every Jew. If we can get into it properly, we will discover a light that increases from day to day, inspiring us to rededicate ourselves and our communities, creating lives of illumination, with a brightness that lights up the world.

THE LONG VIEW

"On the 25th of Kislev (begin) the days of Chanukah, which are eight, on which one may not eulogize or fast. For when the Greeks entered the Sanctuary they defiled all the oil that was in the Sanctuary, and when the royal Hasmonean family (the Maccabees) defeated them, they searched and found only one flask of oil that was sealed with the seal of the High Priest. It contained only (enough) oil to light the *Menorah* for one day, but a miracle occurred, and they lit the *Menorah* with it for eight days. Another year, they established these (days) as Festivals to say Hallel and give thanks."

Shabbos 21b

The Sages established these days as a holiday "another year," *leshanah acheres*, at a later time. Why did they delay?

One reason for the delay was that the Chanukah miracle took place long before the war was ended. The Maccabees had liberated Jerusalem, but the final victory and a peace treaty were not forthcoming for another 20 years, so it was some time before the

Sages made Chanukah a permanent part of the calendar ("another year" after they had gone out from under the hands of the servants of Greece to become servants of Hashem" — *Sfas Emes*).

This explains the delay; but it does not explain why the Gemara, which is always so concise, took the trouble to mention it. Since the Gemara felt if necessary to record that Chanukah was not established immediately, it means that there is some lesson to be learned from this (this holds true even if "another year" means the very next year following the miracle, and the Sages waited 12 months to establish Chanukah rather than immediately create the new holiday).

The lesson is: We should not rush to evaluate the significance of an event until sufficient time has elapsed to provide us with some perspective.

In 1860, one of America's most prominent orators and respected teachers, Henry Ward Beecher, said that future generations would look back at the two greatest heroes of the 19th century: Toussant L'Ouverture and John Brown. Today, few people have ever heard of Toussant L'Ouverture, and the few more who know of John Brown remember him as a murderer and probable psychopath whose aborted slave revolt helped ignite the American Civil War.

In 1963, after President John F. Kennedy was assassinated, a movement began in West Virginia to change the name of the state to the State of Kennedy. Five years later the proposal had been long forgotten, and with more recent biographies bringing to light President Kennedy's true character, the thought of naming a state after him sounds ludicrous.

I was in *Eretz Yisrael* shortly after the liberation of the Old City of Jerusalem during the Six Day War of June 1967, and there seemed to be two groups of people: those who believed that the Final Redemption was just around the corner, and those who believed that the Final Redemption had already arrived. Some seriously questioned the relevance of continuing to mourn over the Exile, and other suggested changes in the *siddur* to conform to the "new realities." We still await Mashiach's coming daily, but the rosy optimism has faded, and few Israelis are confident that permanent peace is at hand.

After the Gulf War and America's victory in Operation Desert Storm in 1991, President George Bush's approval rating was so high that his reelection was taken for granted. Several months passed, and President Bush was out of a job. This is a phenomenon we experience all the time and yet quickly forget: In times of excitement we view a situation in a particular way, but the passing of time soon provides us with a very different view.

Recognizing the natural human short-sightedness can be a lifesaving insight for any parent. The blessing of children brings many problems in its wake, and at some point in a child's development mostly every parent has thoughts of giving up in despair. But children are human beings in formation, not yet finished. If you are stirring the ingredients for chocolate cake in a mixing bowl, you do not see the appeal of the finished product right away. Hashem has a timetable for completing His project, which may extend over many years, and we must learn to take the long view.

Fifty years ago, Orthodox Judaism was declared terminally ill, while non-Orthodox and secular Jewish movements were thriving. Today, even secular Jews admit that only Torah will insure Jewish survival, and they are searching for ways to obtain the Torah's blessings without its obligations, which of course cannot be. Hashem has the big picture, and we little folks should not worry excessively if the tiny reality sliver we see looks gloomier than we would like.

And therefore, even after the miracle of the *Menorah*, after an event that excited the entire Jewish world, even so: "*Leshanah acheres*, another year," *only at a later time* did the Sages institute the holiday of Chanukah. They established Chanukah only after they had the chance to see that the inspiration of Chanukah would stand the test of time, that it contained a message for every generation, even after the Maccabees were conquered by Rome and the Sanctuary itself was destroyed.

In the fast-food throw-away society we live in, one must wonder: If the miracle of the *Menorah* were to occur today, and the Sages waited a few years to decide whether to establish

Chanukah, would anyone by that time still remember that the miracle had ever occurred?

An American artist once made a prediction that "someday, everyone will be famous for 15 minutes." Today's superstar is tomorrow's has-been; today's computer is tomorrow's antique; society gets excited over this week's hit song, this month's best-selling book's this season's style of dressing and acting and even thinking: and it all changes, year to year and day to day. The hectic pace inundates us with so much information of every sort that we become incapable of mentally digesting the changes that occur.

We can absorb all this data only superficially. In the process, we become superficial people, with shorter attention spans and lower thresholds of boredom. What are the implications for serious Torah learning, which demands concentrated attention and long hours which are not always "fun" (*lashon hakodesh*, classical Hebrew, does not even have a word for "fun")? What are the effects on our *mitzvah* observance, and on feelings of holiness in the Jewish heart, when we have lost the ability to think deeply, or the ability to feel connected to unchanging values which are eternal?

Leshanah acheres, the Sages waited; time enough to think about the Chanukah miracle, and time enough to savor the memory of the event as it aged like good wine, and only then did they proclaim the Festival. That should serve as a reminder for us, especially as we celebrate Chanukah, that we must allot some quiet time to ourselves, to look back at all the important things and not allow them to slip away from our memories and our lives.

After lighting the *menorah*, many people spend a few minutes in song or saying *Tehillim* as they bask in the glow of the Chanukah lights. It is also a good time to take a moment to consider the long view, to look back on our past and to ask what are our goals for the future; so that *leshanah acheres*, in 10 or 20 years when we look back at today, we will remember the celebration as one which inspired us to think about eternal values; not to forget, and to live with the *simchah* of knowing that eternal values are the solid bedrock on which we build our lives, and our light-filled homes.

PERIPHERAL VISION

Rav Kahana said: Rav Nassan bar Manyumi expounded in the name of Rabbi Tanchum: A Chanukah light that was placed above 20 *amos* (about 38 feet) from the ground is invalid (above 20 *amos* the eye does not notice it — *Rashi*).

Rav Kahana also said: Rav Nassan bar Manyumi expounded in the name of Rav Tanchum: What is the meaning of the verse (regarding the pit into which the brothers threw Joseph), "And the pit was empty; there was no water in it"? From that which it says, "the pit was empty," do I not know that no water was in it? But by saying, "there was no water in it," it comes to teach that water was not in it, but snakes and scorpions were in it.

Shabbos 21b-22a

Teachings in the Gemara were not recorded haphazardly. When we find two lessons on two very different subjects, even if they were taught by the same Sage, we should assume there is some thematic connection between the subjects themselves (Rav Yerucham Levovitz *zt"l*). But what possible connection is there between proper placement of Chanukah candles and the pit with snakes and scorpions?

I was once privileged to hear the following answer from Rav Moshe Feinstein *zt"l*. A 40-foot-high Chanukah *menorah* is obviously visible, but it is invalid because "the eye does not notice it." It is our nature to focus our gaze on what is in front of us, while something standing in plain sight on the periphery, a little too high or to the side, may not be noticed at all. This is Rabbi Tanchum's first teaching, as it applies to the *Menorah*, or to the maximum height of the *s'chach* of the *succah*.

Rabbi Tanchum then teaches us a second lesson which is an extension of the first: Just as we tend to overlook whatever is not in front of us physically, so too do we tend to overlook that which is not in front of us *emotionally*. In focusing on our interest of the moment, we may overlook something vitally important which stands before our eyes. The proof for this lies in the story of Joseph.

Joseph's brothers hated him and wanted to do away with him, but they acquiesced with Reuven's suggestion when he said: "Do not commit bloodshed; throw him into this pit in the desert, and do not lay a hand upon him." Throwing Joseph into an empty pit to die of hunger and thirst was not far from bloodshed, but the brothers did not want to commit an act of open murder.

However, this particular pit was not completely empty. Like many others in the desert, the pit had become a home for snakes and poisonous scorpions. To lower Joseph into such a pit would be tantamount to open murder, the straightforward bloodshed the brothers wished to avoid. But because of their intense desire to be rid of Joseph, the brothers did not think. Experienced shepherds all, none of them would have climbed into an empty pit without first checking for dangerous denizens. But their emotional focus caused them to overlook whatever facts lay at the periphery, even if (or especially if!) those facts made a mockery of what they hoped to accomplish.

"The pit was empty," is what the brothers saw. "There was no water in it" — but there were other things — is what they could have seen, had they made the effort to notice. Joseph was saved by Divine protection, but the brothers certainly did not expect that to occur, and the Torah holds them responsible.

Most of us are not throwing our relatives into desert pits, but there are nonetheless many snakes and scorpions we overlook. How often do we let slip a harsh word or an embarrassing criticism without asking ourselves: What will be its impact on the other person? When we are focusing on someone's else's failing, or on our own anger, we do not stop to think: Do I truly want to make this stinging remark, which the other person will remember with bitterness for decades? Is it worth my venting my emotions if the person will take their resentment of me to the grave? This happens all the time, and we all know of it from experience with others and with ourselves. But we do not pay attention to what lies outside our field of vision, and we can end up paying a terrible price.

There are many important ideas to think about when lighting the Chanukah *menorah*: fulfillment of the *mitzvah*, remembering the miracles, giving thanks for the blessings and so on. But when setting up the *menorah*, putting it in place and preparing the candles or wicks and oil, there is also an idea worth contemplating: The *menorah* must be placed where people can see it; and even if it is in plain sight, it must not be placed too high, because people do not notice things that lie outside their field of vision.

And therefore, as we prepare the *menorah* each day, we can also remind ourselves: We all tend to overlook important things that escape our notice. We can learn to be more charitable in reacting to thoughtless treatment we receive from others, and we can learn to become more sensitized to the way we treat others in return; expanding our field of vision to include the full height and depth of people around us, to perceive their true needs and to be able to light a candle to illuminate their lives.

THE TZADDIK'S TEMPTATION

With all the joyous celebration of Chanukah, it is sobering to consider that the Chanukah story ended in great tragedy for the victors. Four of the five Maccabees brothers were killed in the war. The sole survivor, Shimon, was not successful in educating his children to follow Hashem's ways, and his son and successor become a Sadducee. A century later, when Rome took over the country, the Roman puppet ruler Herod murdered every man, woman and child of the Maccabee family, so that no descendants remain.

Surely there is a reason why Divine Providence permitted this to occur; and the explanation given by the Ramban in his Torah commentary is that the Maccabees died because they transgressed the law of the Torah. Our father Yaakov said, in *Parashas Vayechi*: "*Lo yasur shevet miYehudah*, The scepter (of royal authority) shall not depart from (the Tribe of) Judah" (*Genesis* 49:10). This is not only a blessing, but a command: A Jewish monarch is not to come from a tribe other than Yehudah. The Maccabees were *Kohanim*, from the family of Levi. They were *tzaddikim*, and great heroes; but their assumption of the throne was a transgression, for which they paid with their lives.

One might ask: Didn't the Maccabees read the *Chumash*? They were true *tzaddikim* (as we say they were in the prayer *Al HaNissim*); didn't they know, or didn't they listen to others, who told them that taking royal power for themselves was forbidden? There is the famous aphorism by Lord Acton, that "power corrupts, and absolute power corrupts absolutely." But if, Heaven forbid, the Maccabees were so easily corrupted, the Creator would not have made them the agents for Divine miracles.

If the Maccabees sinned, it was the sort of sin a *tzaddik* might commit. But what would lead a *tzaddik* to go against an open statement in the Torah?

The answer is: A *tzaddik*, a truly righteous person, seeks only to do good. But the test of righteous people is that sometimes, they want so much to do good that even if their goodness is not the right thing to do, they will do it anyway.

We find in *Tanach* that in the period of prophets and righteous kings, the Jewish people were more than once swept by a wave of *teshuvah*, national repentance. But even in those times, "*rak habamos lo saru*, only the private altars were not taken away" (*II Kings* 15:4, 35). The people repented from every sin, except that they continued to bring sacrificial offerings to Hashem on *bamos* (private altars) in their own backyards, which is forbidden.

Think about it: Whatever the sins of American Jewry may be, I have never seen Jews sacrificing goats in Brooklyn or Manhattan, and not even in Pittsburgh. How is it that the whole people of Israel repented, and yet they kept bringing offerings in a forbidden fashion?

I had the privilege to hear the answer from Rav Moshe Feinstein *zt"l*: The people were righteous, and they desired spiritual elevation (*sheleimus*, perfection, was the word Rav Moshe used). They desired this so intensely that they could not wait to bring the offering to Jerusalem; they had to offer it now, in Bnei Brak or Haifa or Beersheba, even if the Torah forbade it. Their desire to do good, but unaccompanied by the correct perspective according to the Torah, led them to sin.

In the same way, we can explain that the *Chashmonaim*, the Maccabee family, were motivated by an intense desire to serve Hashem and save the people of Israel. They wanted so much to help, and they were convinced that no one else possessed their skills and their dedication. Their evaluation may have been correct. But that altruism itself is what tricked them into concluding: "We are in an emergency situation; no one from the family of Judah is qualified to lead, so we must take power ourselves."

Exactly how they should have reacted, for the details on how they should have selected a leader from Judah, we would have to further consult the commentaries of Ramban and others. But for us, the general principle is: Every *tzaddik* faces the temptation of a *taivah*, a powerful urge, to do good. If the *tzaddik* is not careful, that urge will lead him astray, as surely and as destructively as any other.

Today there are many well-meaning individuals and organizations who seek to make the world a better place. In some cases, the altruistic facade is only a cover for ego, people who want to show that they know best and it is they who will be the community movers and shakers. But often, communal workers truly are motivated by idealism *leshem shamayim*, for the sake of Heaven. Even so, they must still beware of the dangers of becoming carried away by idealism, to the point that they end up doing more harm then good.

When secular Jewish organizations lead the fight against any crack in the government wall separating church and state, they may be inspired by noble motives. But when they end up battling all state aid to Jewish day schools, including even aid to disabled children, then one wonders if the rush to do good has not led them to go overboard.

Even the alleged kidnapping of Yemenite children by Israeli authorities to transfer them to secular homes in the 1950s may have been motivated by a desire to do what the authorities believed was in the children's best interest. But without the Torah's guidance, the most philanthropic desires can be perverted to the greatest cruelty. Even the most selfish people have consciences that place limits on how much harm they will do. But people motivated by misperceived idealism have no such limits, and with their conscience clear they can destroy the entire world (*Rav Yerucham Levovitz zt"l*).

Mitzvah-observant Jews are not immune to this disease. To the contrary, their stronger idealism can place them in situations where they are more likely to succumb. How many *shuls* are racked by *lashon hora* and *machlokes*, slander and dissension, because individuals feel that there is some principle at stake? How many yeshivos have split, or even shut their doors, because idealists convinced of the superiority of their methods of teaching or guiding felt compelled to fight to the bitter end? Idealism is enormously powerful. Misguided, it causes enormously powerful harm.

What is true for the community as a whole is also true for an individual, especially an individual who is a concerned member of a family. A mother seeks to help her son, and a wife seeks to help her husband, but she says: "I want for his good, and I have nagged the daylights out of him for years, but he doesn't change. I even complained to the *mechutanim* (in-laws), and he still doesn't listen!" The intent may be praiseworthy, but one must also consider the drawbacks of adopting the strategy of bulls in china shops.

There was a rabbi who was known for his meticulous observance of the *mitzvah* of Chanukah lights. He always took care to light at the exact moment to fulfill the *mitzvah* in the best possible manner. One Chanukah morning he informed his wife that the proper lighting-time that day was at 5:30 p.m., and asked her if she could be home and ready at that time. She cheerfully agreed. The rabbi left for the day, and he returned with a student at 5:15, coming home to an empty house.

The rabbi prepared the *menorah*, opened the *siddur*, 5:30 came and went, but his wife had still not returned. The student said, "Rebbi, you can light even if your wife is not here"; but the rabbi waited. Finally, at 6:15, the rebbetzin walked in. Her husband greeted her with a smile, and asked if it would be convenient to now light the candles. She said, "Fine, just give me a moment to change." And the rabbi waited five minutes, ten minutes, fifteen minutes, until his wife re-appeared. And then he kindled the *menorah*, an hour late, without any change from his usual demeanor of benevolent *simchah shel mitzvah*.

The student who witnessed all this knew that the rabbi was not timid, and when they were alone he asked: "Rebbi, you are always so strict about lighting on time. How could you delay a whole hour?"

The rabbi explained: "The Gemara says that if a poor person has only enough money to purchase either Chanukah candles or Shabbos candles, he should purchase candles for Shabbos. Although Chanukah candles fulfill the important *mitzvah* of *pirsumei nisa*, publicizing a miracle, Shabbos candles create *shalom bayis*, an atmosphere of harmony in the home, and *shalom bayis* takes precedence. If for *shalom* we will sometimes cancel out the *mitzvah* of Chanukah lighting entirely, then surely the halachah is that for *shalom* it is worth waiting an hour or more."

We must be wary of deciding practical halachah based on stories of rabbis and their rebbetzins. But *Tehillim* tells us: "*Chesed v'emes nifgashu, tzedek v'shalom nashku*, Kindness and truth have met, justice and peace have kissed" (*Psalms* 85:11). Peace without justice is not *shalom*; and truth without kindness is not the ultimate truth, not the Almighty's *emes*.

The correct decision in any particular case demands careful study, and consultation with others who are not involved and who are more knowledgeable. But in general, we should not allow the tragic lesson of the Maccabees to be lost. We should not forget that goodness is a powerful medicine whose doses must be carefully measured, so that good people can make their true contribution, helping to build a greater good for the honor of Hashem, and the benefit of all of *klal Yisrael.*

MORDECHAI'S CHILDREN

Every Jew who is familiar with the *siddur* finds certain paragraphs or phrases that speak to him or her with special power, sending a thrill or a shudder that strikes like a jolt of electricity. For me, the one phrase that hits home above all others is in the *Selichos* prayers for *Taanis Esther*, the Fast of Esther, the day before Purim.

In the *haftarah* (*I Samuel* 15:1-34) for *Parashas Zachor*, the Shabbos before Purim, we read how *Saul Hamelech*, King Saul, was commanded to wipe out the wicked nation of Amalek, even to destroy their sheep and cattle. But King Saul rationalized, he made excuses, and he did not complete his *mitzvah*. *Shmuel Hanavi*, the prophet Samuel, confronted the king, and King Saul said, "*Hakimosi*, I fulfilled the *mitzvah*!" Samuel replied: "*Umeh kol hatzon hazeh b'aznai?*, And what is this sound of sheep that I hear?"

Because King Saul fell short, he lost his crown; and because he did not eradicate the wicked Amalek, centuries later they returned to attack us, when *Haman HaAmaleki*, the Amalekite Haman, issued his decree to wipe out all the Jews.

Haman was against us, and the Gemara says that *Hamelech Achashverosh* King Ahasuerus, was equally against us; and it seems that in Heaven, even the angels were against us. The Jewish people fasted and prayed, but there was very little hope. Until ... it says in the *Selichos davening* we recite on *Taanis Esther*, that Hashem said: "*Umeh kol hatzon hazeh b'aznai?* And what is this sound of the sheep that I hear?"

It means the sound of the Jewish children. And Hashem said, I must intervene, and He arranged for Achashverosh to turn against Haman, and for the whole miracle of the story of Purim.

Hashem saved us because of the voice of the children. The language is very powerful: *kol hatzon*, the sound of the sheep, the same expression which was used by Samuel to condemn was now used by Hashem to defend. Since the words are identical, it is clear that there is some connection between King Saul's failure and what Jewish children did in the time of Mordechai. What is the connection?

The Gemara says that after Haman made his evil decree, Mordechai sat down to study Torah with Jewish children; and together they learned the *mitzvos* in the Torah of *korbanos*, offerings brought in the *Beis HaMikdash*, the Holy Temple in Jerusalem. At that time, the *Beis HaMikdash* had already been destroyed, and the *mitzvah* had no practical relevance. But the Gemara (*Megillah* 16a) says that in the end, Haman himself said: The power of your study session is what foiled my plan.

The meaning is as follows: Centuries before, King Saul was given his *mitzvah* to eliminate Amalek, but he rationalized. He said, Yes, it's a *mitzvah*, but perhaps this particular detail does not apply, and here we can make an exception, and there we can make a modification, and the end result was that the *mitzvah* did not get done, and Amalek returned to haunt us.

Now, in the shadow of a holocaust, Mordechai and the children sat down to learn Torah, and the section they were up to dealt with *korbanos*. It would have been easy to say, "This is not relevant today. We don't have a *Beis HaMikdash*, and who has time to learn Torah anyway, when we have to find a way to oppose Haman!" There were many good excuses not to learn the *parashah*, but Mordechai, who himself was descended from the family of King Saul, learned from his ancestor's mistake. No excuses, no exceptions; this is today's *mitzvah*, let us learn what we can and do the *mitzvah* we have, here and now. And to this Hashem said: "*Umeh kol hatzon*, And what is this sound of the sheep? The Jewish children are learning Torah? I must step in."

And why were the children learning, more than anyone else? Perhaps because the grownups were busy worrying, and trying to make plans for the future. But children know that they can let their parents do the worrying, and they can focus on what is truly important, the *mitzvah* here and now.

Many of the most serious Jewish problems appear to have no solution. American Jewry is rapidly disappearing through intermarriage and assimilation; the Israeli government gives in to its enemies and is still denounced by the world, and innocent children are murdered by terrorists in the heart of Jewish neighborhoods. With all our Jewish talent and all our organizations, it seems as if nobody has the answer, as if the only way we can be saved is through Divine intervention. And that is exactly the point.

In every situation we are obligated to act, to do whatever we can; but Jews must never forget that in the end (and the beginning, and the middle too), everything is in the Hands of Hashem. Purim, and Mordechai's children, are a reminder that the only thing we truly control is our own free will, to choose to do today's *mitzvah*, here and now.

For several years a local *yeshivah ketanah* was housed in a building that is part of our *shul*. At recess time, the children would exit the building through a back door, into the playground. The door would lock behind them automatically, so a child would take a stick to prop the door open to be able to get back into the building. When I saw this happening, I used my key to unlock the door. But the children did not know it, and for days they continued to wedge a stick in the door to keep from being locked out, never realizing that the door was open for them the whole time.

Klal Yisrael faces many, many locked doors, and it is frightening to feel so utterly helpless. But to know that Hashem is in charge, and that He has a plan, and that He will open all the doors in His own time, that is what allows us to sleep at night, and to celebrate *simchos* by day. "The Holy One, Blessed is He, prepares the healing before the wound," and the door is already open in ways we cannot yet see. But by doing our part, without excuses and without delay, we know that Hashem will hear the voice of the sheep, and send his deliverance to us and all the world.

A HOLIDAY FOR NONBELIEVERS

We celebrate Purim to thank Hashem for saving us from the wicked Haman. But the people of Israel lived through other times of national danger, and experienced other miracles of Divine intervention, which are *not* celebrated or even commemorated today. The miracles of Hashem splitting the Jordan and collapsing the walls of Jericho for Joshua, the Heaven-sent plague that destroyed the Assyrian army besieging Jerusalem, those miracles are not marked by festivals, and many people are hardly aware that they ever occurred. Why was Purim chosen for a spot on the Jewish calendar?

We know that a Yom Tov is more than merely a time to remember the past. Each Yom Tov also has its particular message, its special lesson to teach us in the here and now. The Divine destruction of the army of Assyria was an awe-inspiring event; but the *lesson* of that event can be learned from the story of Pesach, and therefore a new Yom Tov was not required. The Purim story is considerably less spectacular; but the *lesson* of Purim was new, and its celebration was therefore added.

What was the new, unique lesson of Purim?

Throughout the books of the Torah, the prophets criticize Israel for every sort of sin. You name it, some of us did it, and the prophets were never shy about calling us on it. It is therefore all the more startling that, in the entire *Tanach*, we do not find that any Jew was ever accused of denying the truth of the Torah itself. Even wicked kings like *Achav* — King Ahab, who worshipped idols and murdered prophets — believed in the Torah. Because, it was impossible *not* to believe.

The nation of Israel possessed the original *sefer Torah* in Moshe Rabbeinu's handwriting, and the Tablets of the Ten Commandments given directly by Hashem. They possessed a jar of *mon*, the original manna. They had national monuments at the place where Moshe had split the Red Sea, where Joshua split the Jordan, and where huge stones rained down from the skies upon their enemies. They had prophets, who could predict the future with 100 percent accuracy. Being human, some people sinned; but everyone believed.

But after our nation was conquered, and exiled and scattered; after the Holy Temple was demolished and the great national symbols were lost; after prophets and prophecy came to an end; then, for the first time, it came more difficult to believe. As Rav Yisrael of Rizhin *zt"l* said, We today are holding on to a rope of faith, but the rope is shaking, violently. What will help us to hold on?

In my wife's family, there is a beautiful Jew whom everyone calls Uncle Lotsy. Uncle Lotsy was born in Czechoslovakia, and in the Second World War he spent time in a Russian Prisoner-of-War camp. He told me how the hungry prisoners spent hours upon hours talking about food: "Someday, when I get out of here, I'm going to sit down to a steak dinner, with onions, and huge tomatoes," etc., going on and on with no greater dream in life than to have their fill to eat.

The Russians finally set Uncle Lotsy and his friends free, on condition that they enlist in the Russian army, which they did. In some ways, it was worse than the prison camp. They suffered through arduous fighting, grave danger, freezing cold — and they were still hungry, most of the time.

In Uncle Lotsy's outfit, the fellow in the next bed was a Jewish communist named Ackerman. Ackerman had been born into an observant Jewish family, but he himself had abandoned religion years ago. Now, in the middle of this hellish existence near the front lines, Rosh Hashanah arrived, and Jewish soldiers in Uncle Lotsy's company were given one day off.

Uncle Lotsy and his friend seized the opportunity to make it to a Rosh Hashanah *davening*. Not Ackerman. He was an atheist, and proud of it. He traveled to the nearest town, called Czernowitz, to pay a visit to the local bar.

Walking through the town, Ackerman suddenly heard a strange sound, a trumpet blowing. Then he realized, it was a *shofar*. The music pulled at him, like a magnet; and he soon found himself inside a little *shul*, clutching a *machzor*. praying along with everyone else, crying his eyes out as much as everyone else, or more.

A few hours later, he told the story to Uncle Lotsy. A few hours after that, the whole outfit went into battle, 200 soldiers. Only seven returned. Ackerman was not one of them.

When his friends heard the news, they said, "Well, Ackerman the communist is dead." There was no one to say *Kaddish* for him, no one to know that he died not as Ackerman the communist, but as Ackerman the Jew. To this day, almost nobody knows the truth, except for Uncle Lotsy, and me; and now, you.

As the saying goes, there are no atheists in foxholes. In time of trouble, when we are in pain we cry out, even if we are alone; because instinctively, we know, Someone is listening. Often, even after the soldier climbs out of the foxhole, that knowledge remains with him. In August 1967, a few weeks after the Six Day War, I had the good fortune to visit Tel Aviv and Jerusalem. It was hard to find a confirmed Israeli atheist, that Summer of '67. It was even harder to find a pair of *tefillin*; they were all sold out.

War, personal troubles and national disasters are all potentially effective methods to bring people closer to knowledge of Hashem. But aren't there any simpler, more pleasant methods?

There are indeed alternative methods, and one such alternative is a thoughtful celebration of Purim.

The Megillah does not mention the Name of Hashem, not even once. There are several reasons for this omission, and one reason is the following: In earlier times, when all Israel felt the Divine Presence, there was no Purim, because Israel did not yet *need* it. Only after the loss of the Holy Temple, after national downfall and exile when belief became more difficult and people began to wonder, did Hashem give us Purim.

For a Jew who does not believe, the Five Books of the Torah are a very difficult read. Hashem is the Main Character, active on every page, and the atheist, whether by choice or by upbringing, finds the story hard to relate to on any serious personal level. But *Megillas Esther* is very different. Hashem's Name does not appear, the story itself is interesting and nonthreatening, and the Megillah can be read as history, an ancestral chronicle. As a festival, Purim can be enjoyed as a national celebration, even as (dare we say it?) an atheist holiday.

Except that: Even if Jews who are unaware of any feelings of faith at all read teh entire *Megillas Esther* thoughtfully, the entire they will not be the same people they were when they began. The thoughtful reader will try to picture, what it was like for the Jews — our ancestors our fathers and mothers — to have lived in the days of Queen Esther.

All Jews everywhere are living in the Persian Empire, under the control of Achashverosh. The king delegates authority to the wicked Haman, and Haman decrees death for every one of us. Queen Esther, who (whether or not we knew her lineage) had always seemed to be a kindly person, has become Haman's good buddy, inviting him to private dinner parties. Our leader Mordechai is first on the list to be hanged. And for us and our families, *there is no way out.*

Mordechai urges us to fast and to pray, and everyone runs to pray. We run also; even if we thought we had no faith, we are all running together and *davening* together. Ludwig von Mendelsohn, *head of the Lutheran Church* in Nazi Germany, in 1934 returned to his Jewish heritage, even though the Nazis considered him Aryan. A Haman shakes us up, and he drops us at the door of the *shul.*

We pray and we fast, for three days and three nights. How many have fainted from hunger and thirst, and how many have died? But we do it anyway, because there is no other way. There is still no real hope, except for the intuitive feeling that somewhere (perhaps? surely?), somehow, Someone hears ...

And then, suddenly, the news breaks: Queen Esther is Jewish, one of us! King Ahaseurus has switched to our side! Wicked Haman is hanging on the gallows built for Mordechai. And Mordechai has been transferred from death row to the prime minister's throne!

In an astonishing reversal of fortune, Jews throughout the empire are receiving royal treatment. Anti-Semites are in hiding, thousands of pagans are trying to convert to Judaism, the world has turned upside down! We rush to the streets, all of us dancing, shouting, laughing and weeping, all at the same time. The singing is spontaneous, songs of thanks to Hashem, and of course we sing along, as we laugh and we weep.

Perhaps it was all nothing more than lucky coincidence? Perhaps it was just a lucky break that King Ahaseurus killed Queen Vashti in a drunken rage, and he just happened to choose Esther as the replacement? And the king, who had always hated Jews, happened to be in a good mood to grant Esther's request when she begged him to save us. Maybe it just happened that way?

Maybe. But no Jew dancing in the street, none of us who were there and who lived through it, believes that.

We could logically analyze the Purim story in all its details, in search of proof to demonstrate the presence of Hashem behind the scenes. But had we *been* there, we would not have bothered, no more than we bother to prove the existence of another person who speaks to us in the same room. The experience itself is more than enough. As the Megillah tells us: "*LaYehudim ha'ye'sah orah,* to the Jews there was light," they saw, and they felt the rope of faith grasped firmly in their hands, a rope they and their children could hang on to, forever and a day.

We have since celebrated over 2300 Purims, and the holiday is today more relevant than ever. So many people are confused about their relationship with Hashem and His Torah, how to feel the closeness and to be strengthened by it. Purim opens a door for us, with its *mitzvah* of reading the Megillah twice, even on the most superficial level. As long as we read it looking for some light, letting the story enter our bones by picturing ourselves and our families in that life-and-death situation, then we will come to know: Things did not just happen, there was no coincidence, and there is no coincidence today.

Purim is the day to relive the story, to fast and to pray, to read and to sing, to dance and to feast, and to offer toasts to Hashem with a large glass of wine; to drink a little, and to think a little, conjuring up mental images of what it was like for our families to drink and to sing on that first Purim, so many years ago. And then we will discover that the *orah,* the special light given to Israel, still shines, and the rope of faith is still within our reach; and that Hashem is always with us, helping us to see and to hold on.

MIRACLES OF THE HEART

The *sefer Beis Yehoshua* (Rav Yehoshua Rubin, Lithuania 1908) asks: Of the two Rabbinic festivals, Chanukah and Purim, which one does halachah consider more important? Which one celebrates the greater miracle?

His answer is: Although Chanukah is celebrated for eight days, and Purim for only one, nevertheless, Purim is considered more important. His proof is that *Chazal* commanded us to eat a Purim feast as we do on a Yom Tov of the Torah, but there is no *mitzvah* to feast on Chanukah. I might add a proof of my own, that *Chazal* say that the *Yamim Tovim* will lose their significance at the end of days, with the single exception of Purim. But if Purim is considered the more important day, we need to ask why it is so. In what way was the miracle of Purim superior to the miracle of Chanukah?

Beis Yehoshua answers: In the story of Chanukah, we were threatened by the Syrian Greeks. In the story of Purim, we were threatened by the wicked prime minister Haman — and *also* by the wicked king, Achashverosh. Make no mistake, the Talmud teaches us that Achashverosh was a Jew-hater equal to Haman. His hatred is not mentioned openly in the Megillah, because Achashverosh switched sides in the end. Since he ended up supporting us, and since the Megillah was written while Mordechai was prime minister and Achashverosh still reigned, it is more politically correct to downplay the monarch's involvement in the original decree; but a careful reading of the Megillah shows us that Achashverosh and Haman were a team.

At both the original Chanukah and the original Purim, Hashem saved us with a miracle. The miracle of Chanukah salvation was that Hashem gave the *Chashmonaim* (Maccabees) a military victory over the Greeks. A small regiment of trained soldiers can defeat even the largest untrained militia, and the Maccabees were untrained amateurs far outnumbered by the professional soldiers of the Greek phalanx. For the *Chashmonaim* to defeat trained and more numerous troops time after time was an open miracle, the Hand of Hashem rescuing His people and granting them victory.

The miracle of Purim was different. King Achashverosh had given his full support to Haman's decree to murder all Jews. The Jews of Shushan fasted and prayed for three days and nights, after which Queen Esther risked her life to enter the king's chambers uninvited, to ask the king and Haman to attend her private dinner party. They came to dinner, returned the following night for a repeat performance, and when Achashverosh asked Esther what she wished, Esther begged for her and her people to be saved from the wicked Haman.

Achashverosh had not known Esther was Jewish, and the turn of events took him totally by surprise. To analyze what went through his mind is somewhat complex; but in short, within a few minutes of the news, the king had Haman hanged on the gallows that had been prepared for Mordechai, he appointed Mordechai to be prime minister in Haman's place, and the world turned upside down (the Persian world; the Jewish world turned right-side up).

Beis Yehoshua concludes: The Chanukah miracle was that Hashem changed nature, allowing a few amateurs to defeat huge bodies of professional soldiers. This was followed by a second miracle, another change in the natural world, that a small jar of olive oil burned for eight days. But the miracle of Purim was that Hashem changed *human* nature, by changing Achashverosh's mind; that Hashem took the king who hated Jews and backed Haman, and made it that he would suddenly befriend us and foil the plot.

To change the laws of physics, for a bit of oil to burn eight days, is a miracle. For amateurs to be victorious over a large army is a miracle. But to get someone to change from his deeply ingrained prejudice, to transform Achashverosh from our enemy into our friend, that is the greater miracle, greater that anything that happened on Chanukah. And that is why only Purim has the *mitzvah* of the Yom Tov feast.

Beis Yehoshua goes on to bring support to his position from the Gemara, but the main thrust of his argument is: Hashem sometimes makes open miracles, but He almost never interferes with *bechirah*, human free will. To change someone's *bechirah*, to turn enemies into friends and Achashverosh into a philo-Semite, is the greatest miracle of all.

Perhaps this also explains why Purim will have a unique status among *Yamim Tovim* after Mashiach arrives. When the Torah foretells the Final Redemption it mentions peace, prosperity and ingathering of exiles, but no open miracles, except one: "Hashem, your G–d, will circumcise your heart and the heart of your children, to love Hashem, your G-d, with all your heart and with all your soul" (*Deuteronomy* 30:6). The Purim lesson, that Hashem will even perform the miracle of changing the human heart, is the basis of the miracle of the Final Redemption itself.

With this understanding we can now appreciate the full significance of *mishloach manos*, the Purim *mitzvah* of sending gifts of food to friends and neighbors. Why is this *mitzvah* only on Purim and not other festive days? Some commentators explain that the *mitzvah* is to send gifts not only to close friends, but also to those people with whom we are not so close, those with whom we may have exchanged harsh words, with the goal that *mishloach manos* will bring us back together. As beautiful as Jewish unity and friendship are, why are they given *mitzvos* on Purim more than any other Yom Tov?

The answer is: Purim celebrates the miracle that, with help from Hashem, human beings *can* cast aside longstanding resentment and prejudice, and enemies can be transformed into friends. Remembering what Hashem did in the case of Achashverosh, we send *mishloach manos* to friends and to those who are not-yet friends, confident that Hashem will assist us to all come together as one. If a miracle occurred to make a Jew-hating Persian our friend, can we not look forward to the miracle of Hashem making *kol Yisrael chaverim*, all Jews friends together, all through the year?

MUTUAL FUNDS

"Some say that before Purim one should give one half of the coin of the realm, as a remembrance of the half-shekel that they gave in Adar" (*Rema, Orach Chaim* 694:1).

The original half-shekel is mentioned at the beginning of *Parashas Ki Sisa*: "When you take a census of the Children of Israel according to their numbers, every man shall give Hashem an atonement for his soul when counting them, so that there will not be a plague among them when counting them" (*Exodus* 30:12).

One way to understand this plague, the mortal danger resulting from the counting, is that it is dangerous for any person to be singled out as an individual before Hashem. When Hashem looks at us as a group and He sees so many *tzaddikim* and so many innocent children and so many who are simply too foolish to know what sins they commit, then Hashem is inclined to be lenient with us all. But when one person stands out in the limelight, when one is counted as an individual, then Heaven also examines them individually: "Do you deserve the limelight? Have you lived up to your potential? Do you truly 'count'?" And that Divine examination can be hazardous to one's health.

This may also explain the teaching of the Sages that those who hold positions of *rabbanus*, community leadership, often die before their time (*Avos D'Rabbi Nassan* 22). Besides the ulcers and hypertension that come with the job, anyone in the public eye attracts Divine attention, with results that are not always desirable.

How do we ward off this plague? "Let each one give an atonement for his soul." *Midrash Tanchuma* says that when Moshe Rabbeinu heard this he said, "each Israelite will have to give a *kikar* of silver," a large fortune! But Hashem said, "Moshe, let each one give this amount (a half-shekel)."

How shall we understand Moshe's reasoning, that atonement requires a mountain of silver? And if we can understand Moshe's reasoning, what new insight did Hashem reveal, why does it indeed suffice for each one to give only a small half-shekel coin?

Human beings are complex creatures, and there are many different spiritual levels on which we can be judged. One level of Divine judgment is the personal, my private relationship with Hashem: Do I fulfill my responsibilities as His ambassador on earth? That is a test almost none of us can pass, as another statement in the same Midrash says: "'atonement for his soul' — Moshe was astonished and said, Who is capable of giving redemption money for his soul?"

But we exist also on a social level, social beings who live in a series of interlocking relationships with many other people, and Hashem can judge us on how much we contribute to our communities. However much we are found wanting on the personal level, we can still find atonement by our contributing to the Jewish people as a whole.

But this too is a difficult test, because how many of us truly give enough of ourselves to *Klal Yisrael*? Since all our resources are gifts from Hashem to begin with, can we hope to find atonement by giving less than a mountain of silver?

How can our puny gifts make up for what is lacking in the recesses of the soul?

Hashem answered Moshe: Yes, giving by itself is never enough; because with all that we give there is the ever present danger that we will only intensify the focus on our own petty selves. "See what I have done, how much I contributed, the talent I displayed!" And the cure itself becomes the disease.

And therefore Hashem explained: In addition to contributing *to* the community, there is another spiritual aspect to living, which is to strive to feel part *of* the community. The atonement of the half-shekel was not that you donated so *much*, but that you donated *half*. You gave a part, a part which had meaning only together with the other parts, and which did not have your individual name or picture on it. That is what shifts the focus from the self to the totality of the *klal*, and that is the atonement and elevation (*Ki sisa*, literally, "When you elevate") of the soul.

Most of us are willing to work for the *shul* or the yeshivah or *chesed* organization, but we fall into the trap of agreeing to volunteer only on our own terms. "I am happy to help plan the program, but I cannot work in the kitchen; and you know it's impossible for me to work together with a committee; and you certainly cannot expect my support if the board of directors voted for a position different from mine; and of course you can't expect me to show up on time; and surely you will not ask me to work with Mrs. So-and-So, or Mr. Such-and-Such!"

We all wish to help. But if, instead of contributing whatever half of the shekel happens to be missing, we insist on starting a new shekel of our own, if I insist that my help must always be given only in my own way, then I am not binding myself to the community, not becoming part of the *klal*. And often, that sort of help turns out not to be helpful at all.

A few hours' drive from my home is the National Historic Park commemorating the Battle of Gettysburg. In 1863, General Robert E. Lee led his Southern army into Pennsylvania during the Civil War. Lee was aided by an outstanding cavalry leader, General Jeb Stuart. Stuart took his horsemen on a daring raid, dashing in a sweeping circle around the Union army, and the raid was a smashing success. Except that, instead of cavalry raids, General Lee needed Stuart's horsemen to scout for the rest of the army; and because Stuart acted brilliantly instead of doing what was needed, the South lost Gettysburg and the war.

That same week, Northern General Ulysses Grant won a great victory at Vicksburg, Mississippi, thanks in part to *his* cavalry commander, Benjamin Grierson. Unlike General Stuart, Grierson was not a natural horseman. Grierson had been kicked by a horse as a child, and he hated horses. But when he joined the army and through some bureaucratic foul-up was assigned to the cavalry, he did not throw up his hands and quit in disgust. There was a job that needed doing, it had been given over to him, so he did his best; and his best turned out to be very good indeed, succeeding where his most brilliant opponent had failed.

Of course, far better examples are the Torah leaders of every generation, from Moshe Rabbeinu accepting assignments in Egypt that he did not choose, to heads of today's Torah institutions accepting burdens of fund-raising they did not choose. But they do the work that needs to be done, because they understand, doing this particular work is the specific half-shekel that was assigned by Hashem to them.

We no longer give the half-shekel, but at Purim-time we remember it, because the lesson of the half-shekel still remains: I must make my contribution to the whole; and instead of focusing on what I wish to give, I must ask what half is missing that needs to be filled in.

It is a time to consider how we can volunteer for some community *mitzvah* project that we do not truly enjoy, and which is not at all our specialty, and which is not something for which we would ever volunteer ... except that, there is a need. And because there is a need, we *will* volunteer, at least once: to do something we do not enjoy, some task which offers neither personal gain nor emotional satisfaction, but which demonstrates our inner desire to act without thought for ourselves; adding our efforts to anther person's project, adding our half to another person's shekel, expressing a desire to elevate ourselves as we become part of something greater, a sacred coin in the realm of the King of kings.

LETTER TO A COMMUNAL ACTIVIST

Dear Chaim,

Thank you for your letter. I understand your frustration with *frum* people who criticize the *yeshivah ketanah,* and who use their criticism as an excuse to withhold their support. Perhaps it is some small consolation to know that you and your institution are not alone. There are plenty of people who will find fault with the *mesivta*, the girls' high school, the *kollel* and the *shuls* (including their own), and even more who find fault with rabbis in Pittsburgh, Brooklyn and Bnai Brak.

I suppose an appropriate response is to condemn the critics as mean spirited and small souled, always putting others down and besmirching the honor of Torah. But in their defense, at least some of their criticism is valid. Torah institutions are not perfect, and neither are human beings. The Torah tells us that even Moshe Rabbeinu erred, though whatever faults he possessed were on a spiritual plane beyond our ability to comprehend.

A thoughtful person will always discover imperfections. The test is: Will we allow our desire for the Perfect to stand in the way of appreciating what is merely Good?

The Steipler Rav *zt"l* wrote of a young man who worked hard to perfect his *kavanah* (concentration) during *davening,* but who became so frustrated by his less-than-perfect success that he gave up *davening* altogether. There is always room for improvement, and we should always persist in the attempt; but we will never attain complete perfection in any *mitzvah,* and we should not expect it of others.

When I was still a *bachur* in yeshivah, someone posted on the bulletin board a letter purported to have been written by a rebbi to a yeshivah *talmid.* There was some talk as to whether the letter was authentic and who might the author have been, but I was so struck by its message (equally relevant to yeshivah *talmidim, baalabatim* or any member of the Jewish community) that I made a copy of it. Here it is:

"Not long ago, I met a *talmid* from Yeshivah Emek HaTorah (I substituted a fictitious name for the name of the yeshivah mentioned in the letter), home for *bein hazemanim.* I am sure he did not represent the true Emek HaTorah spirit, for he was full of criticism and bitterness towards the yeshivah. The *Rosh Yeshivah* came in for his share, and I was supplied items, facts, data with times and places, a complete indictment.

"However, I soon saw that the trouble was not with Emek HaTorah; the trouble was with the young man. He had mentally dwelt on some trivial slights until he had become so out of harmony with the institution that he had lost the power to derive any benefit from it. Emek HaTorah is not a perfect institution — a fact, I suppose, the *Rosh Yeshivah* and most of its alumni are quite willing to admit; but Emek HaTorah does supply certain advantages, and it depends on the *talmidim* whether they will avail themselves of these advantages or not.

"If you are part of a *makom Torah,* seize upon the good that is there. You receive good by giving it. You gain by giving, so give sympathy and cheerful loyalty to the institution. Be proud of it. Stand by its *hanhalah* (directors) — they are doing the best they can. If the place is faulty, make it a better place by setting an example of cheerfully doing your work every day, the best you can.

"If put to the test, an ounce of loyalty is worth a pound of cleverness. I pray you, so long as you are part of an institution, do not condemn it. Not that you will injure the institution; but when you disparage the concern of which you are a part, you disparage yourself."

I have heard quoted in the name of the well-known thinker and teacher, Rav Shlomo Wolbe of Jerusalem, that there have been Torah people of outstanding talent and powerful sincerity who nevertheless ruined their own happiness and contributed nothing to *Klal Yisrael,* because they were too strongly focused on the faults they perceived in our public life. Their perceptions were accurate; but focusing on the imperfection caused them to lose perspective, and they were not able to enjoy a healthy constructive relationship with the community of which they were part.

A literary critic once described a book in these words: "The author has produced a gem. Like all real stones, it has its tiny flaws, but that just proves it is natural. It is a jewel, nonetheless."

After reading the Megillah, we all say *Baruch Mordechai,* Blessed be Mordechai! But at the end of the Megillah itself, we read that Mordechai was *ratzui l'rov echav,* "he found favor with *most* of his brethren." The Gemara explains that *some* of his brethren, some of the outstanding Torah Sages, criticized Mordechai. They felt he had become too involved in the daily affairs of the Persian government, pulling him away from Torah learning.

It appears that not all the Sages agreed with the criticism, but enough did to make it worthy of record in the Megillah. So let's ask: On Purim, did those critical Sages say *Baruch Mordechai?* Did they bless him? They surely did, such is the halachah; we may believe that someone has a flaw, and our assessment may even be correct, but that must not block us from praising the good that is there as well.

What if the bad outweighs the good? What if the president or *gabbai* of your *shul* can by no stretch of the imagination be compared to Mordechai? For such cases, the Megillah gives us the example of Charvonah. Charvonah was an accomplice of the wicked Haman, but at a crucial moment he switched sides to support Mordechai. Charvonah backed Mordechai only out of pure self-interest, after he saw which way the wind was blowing. But we benefited from it, and on Purim to this day we proclaim, "*vegam Charvonah zachur latov,* and may Charvonah, too, be remembered for good."

This is one of Purim's many lessons: Learn to see the good, and speak of it, and support it. Purim is a time to strengthen love of fellow Jews, and love does not mean hiding our eyes from problems that exist. But a first step is to make sure we see the positive side and value it fully, appreciating all the goodness that truly is to be found in our *shuls* and schools, in our relatives, in our neighbors, and in ourselves.

BABYLONIAN NAMES —

A Final Word for Yizkor, or Any Other Time of Year

The Torah identifies the 12 months of the year only by number, e.g. *HaChodesh HaRishon,* "The First Month," or the Second or Third. The Hebrew names we use today, like Nissan and Iyar, are later innovations. Part of "Jewish cultural literacy" is to know where these names came from, and why we changed from the Torah's own system of using numbers.

Talmud Yerushalmi (the Jerusalem Talmud) explains that "*Shemos hechadashim alu imanu miBavel,* the names for the months came up with us from Babylon." That means, through all the centuries until the destruction of the *Bayis Rishon* (First Holy Temple), we called the months by number. When *Eretz Yisrael* was conquered and we were exiled to Babylon, we found the Babylonian pagans using names for the months. We adopted their practice, brought it with us when we returned to *Eretz Yisrael,* and so it remains today.

This is difficult to understand. Why should we adopt names used by Babylonian pagans? If you wish to answer that we only adopted their practice of naming months, but the actual names we may have modified to make our own, the question still remains, why change at all? Making this more difficult is that by abandoning the original system of calling months by number we gave up a *mitzvah*! The Ramban writes that the year begins at Rosh Hashanah, and the first calendar month should properly be Tishrei. But we count our months from Nissan, in order to remember the Exodus from Egypt; to thank Hashem by calling Nissan "The First Month in Another Year of Freedom," and Iyar is "The Second Month in Another Year of Freedom," and so on. But if we use names like Nissan and Iyar, don't we lose this *mitzvah*?

The Ramban himself answers: We use names like Nissan and Iyar because of the prophecy (*Jeremiah* 23:7-8): "Behold, days are coming, says Hashem, when they will no longer say, 'As Hashem lives, Who brought the Children of Israel up from the land of Egypt,' but 'As Hashem lives, Who brought up and Who brought back the seed of the House of Israel from the land of the North, and from all the lands where He had dispersed them, and they will dwell on their land.'"

This prophecy refers to the time of Mashiach, when we will return from everywhere to *Eretz Yisrael,* and the magnitude of the miracles at that time will eclipse even the miracles of the Exodus from Egypt. The Gemara (*Berachos* 13a) explains that we will not forget the miracles in the Egyptian liberation, but they will be secondary to the praises we will sing in honor of the Final Redemption.

The Ramban explains: Since the prophet tells us that we will give praise for being saved from all the nations, therefore, when the Jews returned to *Eretz Yisrael* from Babylon, 70 years after being conquered, they also wanted to offer praise. The praise they selected was to call the names by their Babylonian months, to remember, in the words of the Ramban, "*ki sham amadnu umisham he'elanu Hashem,* to recall that we lived in Babylon and Hashem brought us up from there."

A question remains: Granted, it was proper for our ancestors who left Babylon to commemorate their redemption. But for us, 2300 years later, why should *we* still use Babylonian names? Babylon was only one way-station in the journey of Jewish history; and the Jewish commonwealth that the Babylonian Jews created was destroyed by Rome, along with the Second *Beis HaMikdash* (Holy Temple), long ago.

Today, if we wish to use the calendar to recall what Hashem did for us, does it not make more sense to return to the original system of calling the months by numbers to remember liberation from Egypt? Why continue to use names like Nissan and Iyar to recall Babylon?

Perhaps the explanation is: We still use the Babylonian names even though the reasons why our ancestors used them, to express thanks for their freedom and the rebuilding of the *Beis HaMikdash,* are long gone. We still give thanks with those names, in order to make the point that those reasons are *not* really gone; the goodness of Hashem does not get lost.

Hashem did a great kindness for our ancestors, bringing them back to *Eretz Yisrael* from Babylon and giving them the blessings of the Second *Beis HaMikdash.* But then the Romans destroyed it all, and you might think that nothing remains of the kindness, and the blessings are as if they had never been. That is not true.

In the *davening* for Shabbos and Yom Tov morning we say, again and again, "*ki l'olam chasdo,* for Hashem's kindness is *forever.*" That means: Give a child a candy and the child is happy, for now; but in an hour or less that happiness is forgotten and the child wants something else, and the candy is as if it had never been given. But if you teach a child a skill like reading or bicycling, then even when the lessons are over, even years later when the child has forgotten the teacher's name, the benefit of the lessons remains.

Every kindness from Hashem is *l'olam,* eternal, permanent, because His kindnesses are not just for the moment. They are part of a larger plan, to bring about redemption for *Klal Yisrael* and the whole world. We cannot see the big picture, and we do not always appreciate the details of the plan, but one thing we know: *ki l'olam chasdo,* acts of Divine kindness always have some permanent effect.

For instance, the liberation from Egypt left a permanent mark, a spiritual inheritance, so that even Jews who are far from living Torah lives are noted for their feelings of sympathy for the oppressed. Hashem's voice speaking to our ancestors at Mt. Sinai continues to echo ("Every single day, a heavenly voice emanates from Mt. Horeb," *Avos* 6:2), which explains why today's assimilated Jews seek spirituality even in the most outlandish cults, in far greater numbers than their non-Jewish neighbors. The Jew still hears the echo, even if he or she no longer knows its source.

So too in *Galus Bavel*, the Babylonian Exile, Hashem in His kindness did not allow us to lose our identity and vanish completely, and in the end He brought us back to *Eretz Yisrael;* that created a permanent spiritual power, so that the Jewish people will never disappear. The core of the nation will always endure, and in the end we will reestablish ourselves in *Eretz Yisrael.* This spiritual strength was granted to us as a Divine gift in the Babylonian Exile. We continue to thank Hashem for it by using Babylonian names for the months, to remember, "*ki l'olam chasdo.*"

And just as acts of Divine kindness have a permanent impact on the world, so too human kindness, sincere acts of devotion and sanctity also have a permanent impact. Rabbi Avraham Reiss, Gershom Seixas, Isaac Leeser, Morris Raphall, and Dov Ber Illowy were spiritual heroes who fought for the Torah in 19th-century America against all the forces of assimilation. Of their institutions, descendants, and disciples almost nothing remains, and few Jews today have even heard their names. But Rav Yaakov Kamenetzky *zt"l* said that those Jews who tried to build *Yiddishkeit* in America in the early days with no apparent success, nevertheless laid the spiritual foundation, and all that came afterwards is build on it.

The same is true in our own families. Of the millions of Jews who immigrated to the English-speaking countries, countries where they were subjected to overwhelming economic and social pressures, what percentage of their descendants continued to be *mitzvah*-observant Jews? Why are you one of the select few who was fortunate enough to be among those who uphold the banner of the Nation of the Torah?

One answer is that you are here in the merit of your *mishpachah*. Either your parents were special people, or you had a grandparent or great-grandparent, a *bobbe* somewhere in the past who said *Tehillim* (Psalms) for her children, and she wept. Those tears did not get lost, and the prayers were answered, if not in her generation, then in yours.

Even among *geirim,* sincere converts to Judaism, in very many cases we find that they had a Jewish ancestor, sometimes unknown to them until after they convert; or some other merit, as the Sages tell us that the ancestors of the righteous Ruth included King Balak, who brought offerings to Hashem (albeit for an improper reason), and King Eglon, who honored Hashem by rising from his throne.

Every goodness has its effect. And this is why we continue to use the names Nissan, Iyar, Sivan and Tishrei, to proclaim that Hashem's kindness of old did not get lost. This is also a reason why we say prayers of *Yizkor,* to proclaim that the good deeds our parents did, for Hashem and for their children, continue to live.

We should not depart from a Yom Tov without taking something with us, some mental picture or idea that can continue to inspire. One idea to take along is a resolve to not allow our old memories to grow stale. Every time we take note of a date on the Jewish calendar, that is a good time to bring to mind the acts of kindness Hashem did for us, and the acts of kindness that other people did for us, even in the distant past. And instead of complaining (aloud or in our private thoughts), "But what have you done for me *lately*?", we should try to retrieve some of the goodness from our memory banks and savor it; and see if perhaps it is possible to take a slice of that goodness, and find some way to pass it on.

This volume is part of
THE ARTSCROLLSERIES®
an ongoing project of
translations, commentaries and expositions
on Scripture, Mishnah, Talmud, Halachah,
liturgy, history, the classic Rabbinic writings,
biographies, and thought.

For a brochure of current publications
visit your local Hebrew bookseller
or contact the publisher:

Mesorah Publications, ltd

4401 Second Avenue
Brooklyn, New York 11232
(718) 921-9000